THE RENAISSANCE

QUESTIONS AND ANALYSIS IN HISTORY

Edited by Stephen J. Lee and Sean Lang

Other titles in this series:

THE RENAISSANCE

JOCELYN HUNT

ROUTLEDGE

London and New York

First published 1999
by Routledge
11 New Fetter Lane, London EC4P 4EE

Simultaneously published in the USA and Canada
by Routledge
29 West 35th Street, New York, NY 10001

Routledge is an imprint of the Taylor & Francis Group

© 1999 Jocelyn Hunt

Typeset in Grotesque and Perpetua
by Keystroke, Jacaranda Lodge, Wolverhampton
Printed and bound in Great Britain by Clays Ltd, St Ives plc

British Library Cataloguing in Publication Data
A catalogue record for this book is available from the British Library

Library of Congress Cataloging in Publication Data
Hunt, Jocelyn.
    The renaissance / Jocelyn Hunt.
        p.   cm. – (Questions and analysis in history)
    Includes bibliographical references and index.
    1. Europe–History–15th century. 2. Europe–History–16th
century. 3. Renaissance. 4. Civilization, Medieval.
    5. Civilization, Modern. I. Title. II. Series.
D203.H86   1999
940.2'1–dc21   98–51897

ISBN 0–415–19527–6

CONTENTS

FIGURES

SERIES PREFACE

Most history textbooks now aim to provide the student with interpretation, and many also cover the historiography of a topic. Some include a selection of sources.

So far, however, there have been few attempts to combine *all* the skills needed by the history student. Interpretation is usually found within an overall narrative framework and it is often difficult to separate out the two for essay purposes. Where sources are included, there is rarely any guidance as to how to answer the questions on them.

The Questions and Analysis series is therefore based on the belief that another approach should be added to those which already exist. It has two main aims.

The first is to separate narrative from interpretation so that the latter is no longer diluted by the former. Most chapters start with a background narrative section containing essential information. This material is then used in a section focusing on analysis through a specific question. The main purpose of this is to help to tighten up essay technique.

The second aim is to provide a comprehensive range of sources for each of the issues covered. The questions are of the type which appear on examination papers, and some have worked answers to demonstrate the techniques required.

The chapters may be approached in different ways. The background narratives can be read first to provide an overall perspective, followed by the analyses and then the sources. The alternative method is to work through all the components of each chapter before going on to the next.

ACKNOWLEDGEMENTS

Author and publisher are grateful to the following for permission to reproduce copyright material:

For written sources: Alison Brown: *The Renaissance* (London, 1988); Evelyn Welch: *Art and Society in Italy 1350–1500* (Oxford, 1997); J. Clements and Lorna Levant (eds): *Renaissance Letters* (New York, 1976); D. Englander, D. Norman, R. O'Day and W.R. Owens: *Culture and Belief in Europe 1450–1600: An Anthology of Sources* (Oxford, 1990).

INTRODUCTION

In the study of 'early modern' history, there is an assumption made that students will know about the Renaissance, even if they are not intending to answer specific examination questions about it. The term is frequently used as an adjective, or linked with other topics of the period: Renaissance government, Renaissance literature, Renaissance science and so on; students are presumed to understand the various implications of the word used as this kind of shorthand. As with many periods and issues of history, views and interpretations established in the nineteenth century are subject to detailed revision.

The problem with the Renaissance is that it is seldom a topic of study in schools before the sixth form. Thus, while many people use the word, there is very little certainty about precisely what it means or to what period it refers. The term is most commonly used when discussing fine art, and it is in this sense that most of us are familiar with it. Yet revisionist historians argue that art was its least important aspect, and the one which was least discussed by contemporaries. The emphasis on art dates back only to the mid-nineteenth century and the writings of Jacob Burckhardt, and we should instead focus on the development of humanism and the classical studies of the universities. The assumption that Florence was pre-eminent is similarly Burckhardtian, since, it is argued, the scholars of the Renaissance were based in Rome, and in the other universities. On the other hand, the names most clearly associated with the Renaissance remain those of artists, and indeed, artists from Florence.

A similar issue arises when the dates of the Renaissance are considered: the most generally accepted period is that of the fifteenth century; but any attempt to consider particular aspects of the

Renaissance leads immediately to a 'stretching' of this time scale. The earliest writings in the vernacular in Italy date from the thirteenth century, and the earliest artists to whom the adjective 'Renaissance' is applied are also thirteenth-century figures. The great artists of the Renaissance were active until the late sixteenth century. As far as literature is concerned, the 'English Renaissance' was only just reaching its peak as the seventeenth century began. The science of the Renaissance, and in particular the developments in astronomy, also takes the focus on to the end of the sixteenth century. Thus the period of the Renaissance appears to stretch with every reference, until it comprises the thirteenth to the seventeenth century.

The purpose of this book is to attempt to put into context what students may already know about the Renaissance. Reading revisionist history on any topic is more difficult if the reader does not know what the ideas are that they are rejecting. It is for this reason that this book begins with the dates of the Renaissnace, and with art, and looks at the supposed dominance of the Italian city states: the traditional view of the Renaissance. Further chapters then consider the other topics to which the term Renaissance is often attached.

It is hoped that students of early modern history, who find the term 'Renaissance' cropping up in their other reading, can use the various chapters of this book to consider whether it is an apt link to make. What were the links between Renaissance and Reformation? Is it possible to identify distinctly 'Renaissance' ideas about government? What significant scientific changes are associated with the Renaissance?

1

THE BEGINNING OF THE RENAISSANCE

BACKGROUND NARRATIVE

Major changes took place in many aspects of intellectual life in Europe during the fourteenth, fifteenth and sixteenth centuries. These changes, ranging from technology and astronomy to art and music, share the name the 'Renaissance' because they have been described as a rebirth of concepts and values from classical times as well as the development of new ideas. Although the term was not used till the mid-nineteenth century, Italian contemporaries talked about a 'rinascita' and were consciously proud that they were renewing the culture of their classical ancestors. Historians debate and discuss the significance, the scope, the dating and even the existence of the Renaissance; nevertheless, the word is constantly used as a reference, as an adjective and as a definition of the period. It is therefore important to discuss when the movement began, and for how long it lasted.

For many, the key developments of the Renaissance are those in the field of fine arts. Such people define the Renaissance as beginning with Giotto di Bondone (?1266–1337) whose frescoes – for example, in Padua – display the light, colour and realism associated with the whole Renaissance movement. Until recently, Giotto was also thought to have created the frescoes in the Upper Church at Assisi. Modern scholarship now suggests that these are the work of an anonymous contemporary: the Master of the St Francis Legend; nevertheless, the works certainly demonstrate the same early Renaissance attributes. Others consider that the key artistic development was linear or mathematical perspective, as calculated and used by Filippo Brunelleschi (1377–1446) and by artists ever since.

Similarly, sculpture achieved a recognisably 'Renaissance' style of realism and deep feeling from Donatello (1386?–1466) onwards. The first clearly Renaissance architecture may be seen in Giotto's campanile for Florence Cathedral, designed at the end of his life, and Brunelleschi's classically inspired dome, completed in 1436. At the same time, the painters most famously associated with the Renaissance, and the works which are best known from the period, are those of the late fifteenth and early sixteenth centuries. For example, Leonardo da Vinci's *Last Supper* was painted in 1497, and his *Mona Lisa* in 1504. Michelangelo completed his first *Pietà* (now in St Peter's, Rome) between 1498 and 1499 and painted the Sistine Chapel ceiling between 1508 and 1512; his creative work continued right up to his death in 1564. Thus, if we take the visual arts as the defining features of the Renaissance, we have a movement which developed from the early fourteenth to the mid-sixteenth century.

Extending the term 'Renaissance' to include key developments in literature and scholarship means these dates need to be extended further. The work of Dante Alighieri (1265–1321) may be said to be a mixture of Christian and classical philosophy and imagery. Dante's views about the human and the divine were to be echoed by many writers after him, and therefore many historians would claim him as the first writer of the Italian Renaissance. At the other end of the period, however, there are serious arguments for including William Shakespeare (1564–1616) and his English contemporaries as Renaissance writers also. Their work explores and celebrates all aspects of human life, recognising that individuals can be masters of their own fate and can make their own decisions for good or evil. Although Shakespeare was said, according to Christopher Marlowe, to have had 'little Latin and less Greek', his source materials include classical stories as well as references to the latest events.

Music as a development of the Renaissance also requires an extension of the period beyond the fifteenth century. The Sforza family of Milan hired Josquin des Prez as court musician in 1473, though he soon moved to Rome. However, the name most associated with Renaissance music is that of Claudio Monteverdi (1567–1643),

Plate 1 *The Last Supper* (1495–7) wall painting by Leonardo da Vinci (1451–1519), Milan, Convent S. Maria delle Grazie, Refectory. Photo: AKG Photo

Plate 2 *Pietá*, (1498–9) Michelangelo Buonarroti (1475–1564), St Peter's, Rome. The Vatican, photo: AKG

who developed both church and secular music to a high degree, writing both the first true operas and enduring masses, as well as his *Vespers of the Blessed Virgin* (1610). *MUSIC*

Science, too, developed over a lengthy period. The pioneering work in astronomy done by Nicolas Copernicus (1473–1543) was to be developed and extended by Johannes Kepler and Galileo Galilei well into the seventeenth century. At the same time, discoveries and conclusions reached in anatomy and physiology were to culminate in the publication of works such as William Harvey's *On the Motion of the Heart and Blood in Animals* (1628). *Science*

Historians, since the publication of Jacob Burckhardt's *The Civilisation of the Renaissance in Italy* (1860), have debated the precise definition, origins, dating and significance of the movement, and the two analyses in this chapter consider two aspects of this debate: whether the fifteenth century is the key moment of the start of the Renaissance; and whether it is appropriate to identify Florence, as Burckhardt did, as 'the Cradle of the Renaissance'.

ANALYSIS (1): IS IT REASONABLE TO SAY THAT THE RENAISSANCE WAS A MOVEMENT OF THE FIFTEENTH AND SIXTEENTH CENTURIES?

The publication in 1927 of Charles Homer Haskins's *The Twelfth Century Renaissance* (1) began a debate on the unique nature of the Renaissance which has continued ever since. Haskins discussed the developments of the twelfth century which, he argued, were precisely those which had been used to identify the later fifteenth-century Renaissance: the extension of university education and the interest in and translation of Greek authors. By the end of the twelfth century, Euclid, Aristotle and Ptolemy were all available in Latin, and thus accessible to scholars. At the same time, Romanesque architecture reflected an interest in the building techniques of the classical period, while in the sphere of politics, sovereign states began to develop and to establish their own vernacular systems of government. Roman law became popular, particularly with rulers trying to reduce the power of the barons. Haskins makes the point that these new rulers were delighted to patronise both artists and writers who could enhance their status. Threats to the Church, from heretics such as the Cathars, who based their views in part on careful reading of the Bible, were also a feature, as they were to be of the fifteenth- and sixteenth-century Renaissance. Haskins also referred to economic changes, notably new developments, such as fulling mills, in the production of textiles, to support his view that there was more than one Renaissance.

More recent historians have dismissed the significance of the fifteenth-century Renaissance on the grounds of its limited impact on the population as a whole. Developments are seldom as sudden, or as radical, as at first appears, and changes can be seen as emerging from and merging into one another. Sir Ernest Gombrich, (2) for example, regards it as little more than a change in fashion: after the ornate, complex and symbol-laden art and architecture of the high Gothic period, simplicity, realism and naturalism were to be the 'new look' of the fifteenth and sixteenth centuries.

Burckhardt's perception of the individualism of the artists and intellectuals involved in the Italian Renaissance has also been questioned, as revisionist historians emphasise their reliance on their patrons: when writers described a golden age, with freedom and intellectual excitement for all, they were simply enhancing the social and political position of their patrons. Artists did what their patrons told them to, rather than choosing their own subjects and their own styles, and thus could be seen as retainers in the same way as the followers of the great magnates of bastard feudalism in the North. (3) This is not to suggest that the artists were involved in street violence: the great families also retained unskilled 'bravi' for 'protection'. These historians make the point that artisans obeying instructions have existed in all periods of history, and therefore there is little that is unique about developments in the fifteenth century.

The Italian Renaissance nevertheless continues to be discussed, assumed to exist and written about. As Alison Brown concludes, 'Despite the onslaught of medievalists, modernists and comparative historians, the Renaissance refuses to disappear or lose its relevance. It was a midwife to revolution and also a coherent and wide-ranging movement in its own right.' (4) Evelyn Welch regards 'the fourteenth and fifteenth centuries as both periods of tremendous transition and as ones of remarkable continuity'. (5)

What, then, are the criteria which allow historians to continue to accept the significance of the Renaissance period? First of all, contemporary writers claimed, more than at any other period, that they were living through a golden age, and that the Medium Aevum, or Middle Ages, which separated the great age of the classics from the modern world were now over. They talked about classical learning being reborn, while at the same time describing their world as new and revolutionary. These two centuries saw the recovery of virtually every great classical text which had been lost after the end of the Roman Empire, as well as the adoption of the vernacular for all types of writing other than the most formal government documents. Even the Catholic Church, determined to maintain Latin as the medium of worship, accepted the inevitability of translations of the Bible.

It was during the fifteenth and sixteenth centuries that the use of perspective developed from an experimental technique into a normal part of every artist's education. It is possible that the need for it arose from the developments in architecture: the new, open buildings meant that paintings could be seen from much farther away than when among the columns and arches of Gothic cathedrals, and thus linear perspective became a necessity. No-one comparing paintings of the Renaissance, such as da Vinci's *Virgin of the Rocks*, with late medieval paintings such as the *Wilton Diptych* (both of which are in the National Gallery, London) can doubt that a revolution had occurred in art.

The beginnings of modern physics and astronomy can be seen in the later part of the fifteenth century, as Copernicus argued for a heliocentric explanation of the movement of the planets: this was the first stage in the processes of reasoning which were to culminate with Newton's explanation of gravity 200 years later.

Thinking and education now focused much more upon this world than upon the next. Books about actual and ideal government, schooling and manners were published in Italy, France, England and Germany. Curiosity about the world may have been one of the reasons why voyages of exploration were undertaken at this time over greater distances than at any earlier period.

It may, however, be the case that the most significant development of the Renaissance was not in the field of art, science or literature, but was rather a piece of technology. It has been powerfully argued (6) that the invention of printing with movable type was the single event which sets this Renaissance apart from other, earlier intellectual developments and rebirths. New inventions and ideas were rapidly disseminated across Europe; texts once printed were not subject to errors of copying which could obscure meaning; the comparative cheapness of printed books meant libraries were no longer the sole preserve of the highly educated élite. The invention of printing ensured that Luther had a larger following than John Huss and that Luther's Reformation endured; that Columbus's journeys were followed up by explorers of many different nations, much more than the travels of Marco Polo had been; and that the new techniques developed in Florence and Rome became known wherever artists were employed.

But even if we accept this thesis, the fact remains that it was during the fifteenth and sixteenth centuries that printing began and developed: the decade between the establishment by Aldus Manutius of his press in 1490 in Venice and the end of the century saw three thousand titles printed in Venice, two thousand in Rome and over a thousand in Milan.

The period known as the Renaissance was unique. In its self-awareness, and the confidence and self-congratulation of those active in the fields of art, architecture and literature, it is certainly different from earlier periods of change. The artists of the period are among the best known of Western Europe, and their patrons recognised in a new way that they were promoting works of genius. Above all, the science and exploration of the period changed the perception of Western Europe about the shape of the universe and the world. In turn, printing ensured that the changes and developments were permanent.

Questions

1. What features of the fifteenth and sixteenth centuries made major changes in intellectual life more likely to occur?
2. Why do you think that the word 'Renaissance' is more closely associated with the visual arts than with developments in other fields?

ANALYSIS (2): DID THE RENAISSANCE BEGIN IN FLORENCE?

The components for a successful intellectual movement were all to be found in Florence at the start of the fifteenth century; or it may be the case that historians have examined the features which made Florence exceptional, and calculated that these are the essential preconditions for the Renaissance.

There was considerable wealth: Florence, even after the Black Death of 1348–9, was a populous and prosperous city, of possibly 20,000 inhabitants. (Before the devastation of the plague, its population is estimated to have been 100,000. (7)) The citizens of Florence were active in manufacture, trade and commerce. Textile production was of a high standard, as was metalworking. Florence traded not just with its own hinterland, but over the Alps, and across the seas: near enough the coast for trade, it was safe from the depredations of pirates and corsairs, and Florentine merchants brought back the luxury goods available in the Middle East. The banking predominance of Florence had its base in the papal revenues, which had, over the years, come to be invested in Florence rather than in the volatile and dangerous city of Rome.

Although many of the wealthy citizens of Florence owned estates in the countryside of Tuscany, their surplus wealth was not swallowed up in the true country landholder's obsession with procuring more land: instead, they were able to spend their fortunes on the agreeable luxuries of art and culture. It may be that the reduction in numbers effected by the Black Death left the survivors and their descendants both richer and more eager to enjoy life on earth while time remained to them. F.W. Kent and P. Simons (8) suggest that these wealthy citizens regarded the artists they patronised in much the same way as magnates in Northern Europe perceived their armies of retainers: that is, as an essential indication of their power and status. On the other hand, the work of these artists and architects bears little resemblance to the fighting in which the retainers of 'bastard feudalism' were so often involved. For the rich men of Florence seldom felt the need to 'own' their own fighting men, preferring rather to hire at need skilled mercenaries under contract or *condotta*. The leaders of these mercenary armies found them a source of revenue, rather than an expense. Indeed, *condottiere* such as Francesco Sforza of Milan used the income from their armies to patronise artists in their turn.

The citizens of Florence were proud of their political system, which they compared to those of the ancient Greek city states. Unlike the combined rule elsewhere of king, Church and nobility, in Florence the citizens ruled themselves, either indirectly, by electing the nine men of the Signoria, or by holding office themselves for the two-month term. Committees, appointed by lot, dealt with the various aspects of the administration. The government saw everyone as equal; no-one was above the law and all aspects of life were supposed to be regulated for the good of the whole community. It has been suggested (9) that this way of life became more valued as it came under threat, first in the wars against Milan (in the early fifteenth century) and later when a single family, the Medici, took over control of most of the councils and committees. Florentines looked back with nostalgia to the great days – as they saw them – of their freedom: Michelangelo's statue of *David* (completed 1504) was the result of a city commission to depict the strength and vigour of Florence. The city's decline was the result in part of economic change and recession, with the loss of valuable markets and skills, and in part of over-ambitious and expensive foreign policies, such as the war to capture Pisa (1509). This decline meant that artists moved to find patronage in other cities.

During the second half of the fifteenth century, however, the family of the Medici established their authority over Florence, and employed artists to enhance their status and to demonstrate their commitment to the cultural life of the city. Lorenzo de' Medici invested in art which would immortalise his family, but at the same time make the city of Florence famous. Once noted scholars and artists were associated with a particular city, they would act as magnets to draw others in. Once a great work of architecture, such as the dome of Florence Cathedral, had been constructed, it would be copied elsewhere, most notably in the design and construction of St Peter's, Rome.

The dominance of Florence does not mean that there was no sign of the Renaissance elsewhere, both in Italy and in the rest of Europe. The classical revival was at its strongest in Rome, where the largest number of classical buildings remained to inspire the artist. And there was no patron in Italy able to outbid the papacy when it chose to commission the work of artists. In Ferrara and Mantua, as well as in Milan and Naples, rulers worked hard to attract and inspire the great artists of the Renaissance. Other cities took the lead in other fields: Venice became the uncontested centre of the new printing industry. In Northern Europe, artistic developments appear to have paralleled what was happening in Italy. The sculptures of Veit Stoss and Adam Kraft, the drawings and paintings of Dürer, Holbein and Van Eyck are demonstrations that the fifteenth- and sixteenth-century Renaissance was not limited to Italy, still less Florence.

Nevertheless, it is Florence which is permanently associated with the initial changes of the Renaissance. The combination of wealthy and discerning patrons, a self-conscious pride in citizenship, and an extra-ordinary accumulation of talented men, all these mean that Florence is certain to remain at the heart of any serious study of the origins and development of the Italian Renaissance.

Questions

1. In what ways were the city states of Italy different from other areas of Europe?
2. Were economic or political developments of greater importance in providing the right conditions for the Renaissance in Florence?

SOURCES

1. CONTEMPORARY PERCEPTIONS OF THE RENAISSANCE

Source A: Giovanni Boccaccio (1313–75) on Giotto.

And thus he returned to the light that art which had been buried for many centuries under the errors of those who had painted more to delight the eyes of the ignorant than the intellect of the wise.

Source B: Matteo Palmieri writes in his *Vita Civile* (around 1420).

Before Giotto, painting was dead, and figure painting laughable. Having been restored by him, sustained by his disciples, and passed on to others, painting has now become a most worthy art, practised by many. Sculpture and architecture, which for a long time had been producing stupid monstrosities, have in our time revived, and returned to the light, purified and perfected by many masters . . . anyone of intelligence should thank God for being born in these times, in which we enjoy a more splendid flowering of the arts than at any other time in the last thousand years.

Source C: Marsilio Ficino to Paul of Middleburg, 1492.

So if we are to call any age golden, it must certainly be our age which has produced such a profusion of golden intellects. Evidence of this is provided by the inventions of this age. For this century, like a golden age, has restored to light the liberal arts that were almost extinct: grammar, poetry, oratory, painting, sculpture, architecture, music . . . and all this in Florence . . . where the Platonic teaching has been recalled from darkness into light. In Germany in our times have been invented the instruments for printing books; not to mention the Florentine machine which shows the daily motions of the heavens.

Source D: Erasmus to Aldus Manutius, 1507.

As not only by your skill and the unrivalled beauty of your typography, but also by intelligence and learning of no common order, you have thrown a vast light upon the literature of Greece and Rome, I should be glad if those merits had brought you in return an adequate profit . . . I am told that you are editing Plato in Greek, a book expected with the greatest interest by the learned world.

Source E: Louis le Roy, writing in 1575.

For now we see the languages restored, and not only the deeds and writings of the ancients brought back to light, but also many fine things newly discovered. In this period, grammar, poetry, history, rhetoric and dialectic have been illuminated by expositions, annotations, corrections, and innumerable translations. Never has mathematics been so well known, nor astrology, cosmography and navigation ..., physics and medicine ... arms and military instruments ..., painting, sculpture, modelling and architecture ..., jurisprudence and eloquence, even politics ... and theology. Printing has greatly aided this work and made easier its development.

Questions

*1. Explain the meaning of the term 'Platonic' (Source C). (2)
2. How correct is Erasmus (Source B) in the importance he places on the invention of printing? (3)
3. Compare Sources A and B. To what extent do they agree about the significance of Giotto at the dawn of the Renaissance? (5)
4. Study Source C. How complete an account of the changes of the Renaissance does Marsilio Ficino offer in his letter? (7)
5. Using these sources and your own knowledge, consider the validity of the view put forward by Ernest Gombrich that the Renaissance was little more than a change in fashion in the visual arts. (8)

Worked answer

*1. [For two marks, you can afford to be brief, but clear, showing that you understand both the origin of the word, and its meaning in this context.]

The word Platonic, referring to the Greek philosopher Plato, refers both to a teaching method, involving discussion and the testing of hypotheses by argument, and to a world view which expressed an open-minded curiosity about the world, and the possibility of mankind attaining a higher level of understanding of life.

SOURCES

2. FLORENCE IN THE TIME OF THE RENAISSANCE

Source F: Leonardo Bruni (1369–1444) describes the Constitution of Florence.

The Florentine Republic is neither completely aristocratic nor completely popular, but is a mixture of both forms. This can be seen clearly from the fact that the nobility, who are prominent for their numbers and their power, are not permitted to hold office in this city, and this is contrary to aristocratic government. On the other hand those who practise menial trades and members of the lowest proletariat are not admitted to the administration of the republic and this seems contrary to democracy. Thus, rejecting the extremes, this city accepts men of the middling kind – or rather it inclines to the well born and the richer kind of men, provided they are not excessively powerful ... In the olden days, the people used to take up arms in time of war and fight the city's battles ... Later wars began to be fought by mercenary soldiers. Then the power of the city was seen to depend not on the people but on the aristocracy and with the rich, who provided the republic with money.

Source G: Gregorio Dati explains Florence's prosperity.

One reason is this. Because the city of Florence is situated in a naturally wild and sterile place, no matter how hard it is worked, it cannot provide enough for her inhabitants to live off; and because the population has greatly increased due to the temperate and generative climate of the place, it has for some time been necessary for Florentines to provide for this enlarged population by hard work. So, for some time now, they have gone abroad to make their fortune before returning to Florence ... and travelling through all the kingdoms of the world ... they have in this way seen the customs of the other nations in the world and have adopted what they favoured, choosing the flower from every part; and in order to be able to follow these customs, they have been filled with an even greater desire to see and to acquire ... so that whoever is not a merchant and hasn't investigated the world and returned with possessions to his native home, is considered nothing ... So great is the number of talented and rich men that they are unequalled in the world.

Source H: Giovanni Rucellai, a merchant, 1473.

I have also spent a great deal of money on my house and on the church of Santa Maria Novella and on the chapel with the tomb I had made in the church of San Pancrazio, and also on the gold brocade vestments for the said church, which cost me more than a thousand ducats, and on the loggia opposite my house, and on the house and garden of my place at Quaracchi and at Poggio a Caiano. All the above-mentioned things have given and give me the greatest satisfaction and pleasure, because in part they serve the honour of God as well as the honour of the city and the commemoration of myself.

It's generally said, and I agree with it, that earning and spending are among the greatest pleasures that men enjoy in this life ... I myself, who have done nothing for the last fifty years but earn and spend, as I describe above, have had the greatest pleasure and satisfaction from both, and I really think it is even more pleasurable to spend than to earn.

Source I: Niccolo Niccoli reprimands Piero de' Pazzi.

[Niccolo] asked him what his occupation was, he replied, as do the young: 'Having a good time.' Niccolo said to him: 'Considering whose son you are, considering the good family you come from and your good looks, it is disgraceful that you do not devote yourself to Latin letters, which would give you great distinction. If you do not study the classics, you will be considered a nothing; when you have passed the prime of your youth, you will find yourself without any merit, and you will enjoy no-one's esteem.'

Source J: From the writings of Lorenzo de' Medici.

Two days after the death of my father, although I, Lorenzo, was very young, being only in my twenty-first year, the principal men of the city and the state came to our house to condole on our loss and encourage me to take on myself the care of the city and the state, as my father and grandfather had done. This proposal being contrary to the instincts of my youthful age and considering that the burden and danger were great, I consented unwillingly, but I did so to protect our friends and our property, for it fares ill in Florence with anyone who possesses great wealth without any control in the government

Questions

1. In the context of fifteenth-century Italy explain the meaning of the term 'mercenary' (Source F) (2)
*2. What can you learn from Niccoli's reprimand (Source I) about the social groups most likely to be involved in cultural developments? (3)
3. How complete an account of the motivation of patrons do you think is given by Giovanni Rucellai (Source H)? (4)
4. Study Sources F and J. To what extent do these two sources taken together explain the changes which occurred in the government of Florence, and the fact that the Medici became the rulers of the town? (7)
5. Using these sources and your own knowledge, discuss the extent to which circumstances in Florence provided an ideal base for cultural development in the fifteenth and sixteenth centuries. (9)

Worked answer

*2. It is possible to see that both the speaker and his object are from a small social group, since they know one another. The reasons given by Niccoli to urge the young Pazzi to study seriously are also about status, and position in society. He warns him that he may face an old age without esteem if he does not mend his ways. These are the preoccupations of the wealthy and those with some position in society to maintain, rather than of the ordinary people, whether urban or rural.

2

HUMANISM

BACKGROUND NARRATIVE

Modern humanism stresses the importance of human achievements, with people making their own choices, rather than relying solely on the will of God to fix their status and the pattern of their lives. In the period of the Renaissance, the word humanism denoted a very different intellectual approach. The Renaissance perception was that God had given mankind the potential to achieve a good life, and thus it was the duty of each person to use those talents to the full. Nowadays, the word is often applied to ideas which are purely secular, or non-Christian, so that people who share some of the ideas of humanism, but are Christians, find it necessary to call themselves 'Christian humanists'.

The word was first used in the fourteenth century as a description of the university curriculum in Bologna, to distinguish students who were studying the 'humane' subjects such as rhetoric, rather than law or theology. This meant that it was important to learn from the great deeds of past ages, rather than relying simply on the grace of God. The word humanist therefore defined those scholars who were reviving the classics, who found manuscripts, and translated them, or had them translated. It was applied to those who valued the beauty of properly written Latin and Greek, and extended to those who felt strongly about the importance of education. Of all the key personalities of the Renaissance, it was the humanists who most saw their work as a rebirth of the lost golden age of the classics. Their influence was felt in every aspect of the Renaissance; the contempt that humanists showed for the scholastic methods of the university scholars, rereading and re-annotating the works of the Fathers of the Church, was to be one of the triggers for attacks on the papacy, culminating in the Reformation. At the same time, the demand for accurate and beautiful Latin and Greek also encouraged the textual criticism which was to bring about Martin Luther's definitive critique (1517) of the indulgences which arose from the doctrine of Purgatory, which will be discussed further in Chapter 4. The impact of humanist studies was also felt in art and architecture, in politics and in science.

The initial phase of the humanist movement involved the accumulation of classical texts. Some of the Latin authors had been known throughout the Middle Ages: Ovid's poems, for example, had been used, with the racier passages removed, as Christian morality tales, and the Church claimed that Seneca had corresponded with St Paul. Plato, in Latin translation, had been adopted and 'Christianised' from the time of Charlemagne onwards. Neo-Platonism proved useful to the Church, which adopted Plato's concept of the ideal to describe its view of the perfectibility of mankind through the love of God. The Catholic explanation of the Eucharist, transubstantiation, is a Platonic one. During the twelfth century, in part because of the crusades, many Greek works were recovered. These writings had been lost to the West with the end of the Roman Empire, as the manuscripts disappeared and the ability to read Greek vanished. The Arabs had adopted and studied Euclid, Archimedes and Ptolemy, and these became available in Latin translation in the twelfth century. The thirteenth and fourteenth centuries, however, saw an amazing increase in the number of texts available. Manuscript hunting became a passion, and the libraries of the ancient monasteries were searched to find and save the great minds of the ancient world. Petrarch (1304–74) for example, travelled much of Italy. In the monastery at Monte Cassino, he found pages cut out, or torn out, for use in day-to-day clerical work. It was Petrarch who rescued and publicised Livy's *Decades*. He also introduced Homer to the modern world. He had not learned Greek as a student, but his discovery of a text of Homer was enough to persuade him to find tutors from the Eastern Empire to teach him, and by his death, he had published a Latin version of the *Iliad*. The first chair of Greek in Europe was established in Florence in

1396. Coluccio Salutati, Chancellor of Florence at the end of the fourteenth century, owned as many as 600 books. This was an impressive library, given that the copying of a book by hand took weeks of skilled work. There was such profit in book buying that the Sicilian merchant Giovanni Aurispa made a trip to Byzantium in 1423, returning with 238 books, including the first copies to reach Europe of Aeschylus and Aristophanes, two great playwrights of ancient Greece.

Education was important, if children were to have the intellectual background to seek out the right way in their lives. In Mantua, in the early fifteenth century, the Gonzaga family persuaded the scholar Vittorino da Feltre to run a school, at first for their own children, but soon extended to included seventy children of the town. They were taught reading and writing, Latin and Greek, but also astronomy, geography, and even physical education. These literary, or humanist, schools were different from the 'abacus schools' where merchants' children usually learned the skills they needed, and few merchants' children would progress to the grammar schools unless they were intending to follow a profession such as the law. Elsewhere in Europe, education also developed. The Dean of St Paul's, John Colet, opened a school in London, with a humanist curriculum and approach, and similar schools opened in towns in France and the Netherlands. Colet's view was that it was irrelevant whether teachers were clergy or not, provided they could teach well.

The development of printing was particularly significant in the spread of humanism. From the establishment of Aldus Manutius's press in Venice, the price of books fell dramatically, and the number of copies increased. While classical and humanist writing probably accounted for not more than 10 per cent of the total published, none the less, the number of copies available extended the possibility that even children could be entrusted with books.

Historians have for many years attempted to define the connection between the essentially academic and scholarly humanist movement and the other developments of the Renaissance. The two analyses which follow discuss the extent to which the classics influenced the visual arts, and the question of whether this literary movement was ever more than a limited pastime for the wealthy.

ANALYSIS (1): TO WHAT EXTENT IS IT POSSIBLE TO DISCERN CLASSICAL INFLUENCES IN THE VISUAL ARTS OF THE RENAISSANCE?

'Archaeology was a creation of the renaissance.' (1) It would have been impossible to live in, or visit Italy in the Middle Ages and yet remain ignorant of the classical past. Pilgrims visiting Rome had always been amazed by the size and grandeur of the ruins of the classical period, but there had been little respect for the buildings and other remains themselves. Marble had been 'quarried' from the buildings of ancient Rome to build and embellish the churches of the Gothic period. Cinerary and funerary urns had been 'adopted' as fonts or holy water stoups. Marble walls and statues were crushed to produce lime wash for whitening walls. There were examples of ancient statues being 'renamed' in the Gothic period, and acquiring new leases of life as saints or church fathers. But only with the beginning of the Renaissance do we find the start of systematic archaeology, combined with reverence for the artistic and architectural achievements of the ancients.

Inevitably, the increased interest in the physical remains left from classical times affected artistic developments, both in technique and in content. As early as the second half of the thirteenth century, Nicola Pisano was directly imitating classical forms, for example in his pulpit for the baptistery at Pisa Cathedral, where the supporting figures are carved with a striking realism. The work of Giotto (1266–1337), at about the same time, demonstrates the 'new classicism' of simple lines and worldly detail in pictures of spiritual subjects, though Roberto Weiss may have overstated his case when he claimed that, 'With Giotto the first morning lights of the Renaissance began to appear on the medieval sky,' (2) since Giotto was not making use of the techniques of linear perspective. The application of theory to the business of painting was seen as a part of the rebirth of classical times. To take the best from the past but also to add to it the best of modern times was a central tenet of the Renaissance. By the time the Florentine painter Masaccio died in 1428, perspective was a fully established technique, and this was a new system, unknown to the painters of ancient times.

The subject matter of painting was directly influenced by growing knowledge. Mantegna (1431–1506) studied Trajan's Column in Rome in order to paint his series, *The Triumph of Caesar* (now at Hampton Court). Indeed, some critics have found these pictures cluttered, such is the wealth of authentic detail he included. (3) Botticelli

(1444–1510) also chose pagan themes for some of his greatest works. The patrons of the artists were often depicted in classical pose, or in classical dress, with the rediscovery of the equestrian statue a typical example.

Sculptors found it easy to make direct use of classical examples, since classical statues survived in substantial numbers, and were prized by the collectors of Florence and Rome. Donatello (1386–1466) was inspired by the realism of the ancient sculptors. As a result, his ragged and despairing *Magdalen* produces a reaction of sympathy, in whatever age she is seen. Michelangelo, too, attempted above all to reproduce the actual physical attributes of the figures he carved, from the early moment in his career when he carved and 'aged' a faun which he successfully passed off as a genuine antiquity.

In architecture, the grand simplicity of classical style was adopted and extended, thanks to the advances in technology which character-ised the period of the Renaissance. Leon Battista Alberti, in 1434, expressed his admiration of Brunelleschi's dome: 'What man, however hard of heart or jealous, would not praise Pippo the architect, seeing so vast a construction here, raised above the skies, broad enough to cover all the people of Tuscany with its shadow.' (4) A combination of the structure Brunelleschi had admired in the Pantheon in Rome and the latest in engineering machinery ensured that the dome became one of the wonders of the world, imitated in Rome and, over the next two centuries, as far north as London.

On the other hand, the preoccupations of the fifteenth and sixteenth centuries may also be clearly seen in the visual arts of the period. Religious themes continued to predominate, even if these themes were treated in a realistic and classical way. The Virgin and Child may have been drawn from life, and set in a context of Italian life, but the reverence and piety of the many depictions of the Holy Family are always the key feature of the paintings. Michelangelo may have dissected corpses to achieve anatomical accuracy, but the subject matter he and other artists chose was almost always biblical and religious. Indeed, some of the artists became anxious about the pagan content of their pictures. In his later life, and under the influence of the monk Savonarola, Botticelli expressed regret about the subject matter of his earlier masterpieces, the *Birth of Venus and Primavera*. Savonarola objected particularly to the 'pagan' depiction of Christian scenes, notably the way the Mother of Christ was shown, as if she were rich and shameless.

Religious themes were bound to predominate, since the chief patrons and sponsors of the arts were, as they had been throughout

Plate 3 *The Birth of Venus* (c. 1482) Sandro Botticelli (1445–1510), The Uffizi Gallery, Florence. Photo: AKG/Erich Lessing

the Middle Ages, the princes of the Church. The popes were anxious after the schism of 1378 to 1417 to re-establish their status as leaders of Christendom, and magnificent buildings and great art were obvious ways to achieve this. New and beautiful churches and palaces provided work for the architects and showcases for the painters and sculptors of Western Europe. Those laypeople who sponsored the artists were also, in part, moved by the desire to glorify God, with one eye at least on the future of their souls. At the same time, the humanist view of aspiring man encouraged artists and their sponsors to try new ways of sharing the divine experience of creation and recognising with awe the beauty of God's world.

While much of Renaissance art can be seen as a reaction to the stylistic content of the high Gothic period, on the other hand, the influence of the classical revival is unmistakable. The achievements of the great cathedral builders of the Middle Ages had carried the use of vaulting to its highest level. New styles, and new engineering techniques to make them possible, replaced the soaring spires of the medieval with the domes of the early modern. Similarly, the depth and detail of the Renaissance artists shed new light on the Gospel stories which were their most frequent subject. Renaissance art shows a synthesis of the 'ancient' and the 'modern'. Contemporaries recognised their debt to the classical past while claiming for themselves the genius of the new.

Questions

1. What was the influence of classical myth and legend in the paintings of the Renaissance?
2. How far was the taste of the patron a significant element in the production of works of art in the Renaissance?

ANALYSIS 2: HOW FAR WAS THE RENAISSANCE THE CONCERN ONLY OF THE EDUCATED ÉLITE?

Intellectual developments in any period must be the concern of those with sufficient wealth and adequate leisure to focus on matters other than the simple question of subsistence. It is also likely that such developments will occur in towns, since the free interchange of ideas is an essential component, and the difficulties of communication in the countryside were considerable in any age before our own.

The patrons of the scholars, painters, architects and scientists of the Renaissance were the rich and the influential. The Church was wealthy because it collected enormous revenues from all of Christendom. The people paid tithe, one-tenth of their income, to the Church, and a part of this was forwarded to the diocese, and to the central Curia, in Rome. Other payments were made by the laity, including fees for some ceremonies, and fines for breaches of canon law. Ordinary people might also give land or possessions to the Church at the time of their death, with a view to easing their passage through Purgatory, and by the fifteenth century the Church had begun to make considerable sums through selling indulgences to ease the route to paradise. While some of these revenues were spent in pursuit of the political aims of the papacy, some were spent on the visible glory of the Church.

In the city states of Italy a similar need for status-enhancing buildings and artworks stimulated the patronage of the Medici, the Este, the Sforza and the Gonzaga. These families admitted to wishing to outdo their rivals, in culture as in war, and competed to employ the most noted artists. The money for new buildings and works of art came in part from commerce and banking, and from the substantial profits to be won in the luxury trade of the Mediterranean and Middle East. But revenue was also obtained through taxation. In republican Florence, the decision to commission 'civic' works of art was reached after public debate, with the involvement of those whose pockets would be affected. In turn, the architecture, sculpture and painting of these cities was accessible to all ranks in society. When they attended church on Sundays, when they presented themselves in the town halls and palaces of their towns in pursuit of justice or of commercial decisions, they saw the work of the Renaissance artists all around them. While this is particularly true of the urban classes, the city states were the market towns for the surrounding areas, and thus country folk were also exposed to the latest works of art.

The collection and copying of books was the hobby of the extremely rich. Travellers who had the time simply to search for manuscripts wanted to recoup their costs when it came to selling what they had found. The tiny number of copies in the Western world enhanced the huge value of the great libraries, and they were naturally carefully guarded by their owners. All this changed with the development of the printing press: after all, even the simple presses of Aldus Manutius or William Caxton could produce a thousand copies in the time it would take a human copier to make one. In 1543, over 400 copies of Copernicus's *De Revolutionibus* were produced. The print shops became salons, where the interested met and argued. On the other hand, even five hundred or a thousand copies of a book hardly suggest mass availability or demand. The bulk of early printed books tended to be religious stories, lives of the saints or books of hours, rather than discussions of the incisive new ideas of the intellectuals of the Renaissance.

Education, too, continued to be predominantly the privilege of the few. The royal and noble families of Europe ensured that their children were educated to the highest level. The study of Roman law, and of genius of classical times, could be a weapon in the struggle for power between the Church and the lay authorities. On the other hand, the urban merchant classes of Italy, and of other great cities, educated their children − for example, in the 'abacus schools' − in the skills they would need, and it was a short step from this education to the less practical. Indeed, the Vespucci family of Florence, members of the minor nobility, sent their older son away to university to study the classics, while the younger son, Amerigo, was educated by an uncle in trade and navigation: abilities which were to stand him in good stead.

The humanists believed, however, that men needed to be educated so that they could lead good lives, and in some areas this translated into education for the poor. Where monasteries and parish priests had perhaps taught prayers and the catechism, these schools hoped to teach the children the right values by which to make choices for life. In Mantua, the children of poorer families of the city could attend the school of Vittorino da Feltre paying what they could afford in fees. John Colet's St Paul's School took poor as well as rich children; the poor paid by doing housework at times when they were not engaged in their studies. None the less, these schools were hardly universally accessible. Not only were they an urban phenomenon; they also required families to be prosperous enough to do without the work of their children. While this was more possible in town than in agricultural areas, it was never universally possible. An apprenticeship in some trade would obviously be more directly useful than a liberal education, although the opportunities for prestigious appointments existed if a young man had managed to acquire a good education.

Where men from classes other than the wealthy were able to become scholars, as is the case with the Dutch humanist scholar Desiderius Erasmus (1466−1536), they relied entirely on the patronage of the wealthy to allow them to travel, and to study and write. Erasmus's first trip to Italy, for example, was as tutor to a noble. The travelling scholars of the earlier Middle Ages had been clerics, who moved from monastery to monastery. This pattern was echoed, but with the scholars able to stay in palaces and town hostels.

Academic study in the Renaissance was the province of the few rather than the many. Without the interest and financial backing of the rich, there would have been little opportunity for the accumulation of libraries, for experimentation in art and technology and for the creation of beautiful buildings. The rich did these things for their own pleasure and benefit. But the fruits of Renaissance study filtered down to the ordinary citizens, at least in the self-consciously proud city states of Italy, and the prosperous trading cities of the rest of Europe. And the influence of Renaissance thinking on education, government, religion and science was to have far-reaching effects which were to last well beyond the developments of the next trends in art.

Questions

1. For what reasons did the wealthy and influential classes of Renaissance Europe choose to spend their money in sponsoring scholars and artists?
2. Does the fact that the Renaissance was predominantly the concern of the ruling class make it any less valid as a topic of study?

SOURCES

1. THE IMPACT OF CLASSICAL LEARNING

Source A: Giorgio Vasari about Nicola Pisano (?1225–?85).

Now Nicola Pisano found himself under some Greek sculptors who were working on the figures and other carved ornaments of the duomo at Pisa and of the church of San Giovanni, on the occasion when, among the many marble spoils brought back by the Pisan fleet, were discovered some ancient sarcophagi . . . in a style that was most beautiful, as both the nude and the draped figures were skilfully executed and perfectly designed.

Source B: Vasari's Preface to his *Lives of the Painters*.

For having seen in what way art, from a small beginning, climbed to the greatest height, and how from a state so noble she fell into utter ruin, and that in consequence, the nature of this art is similar to that of the others, which like human bodies have their birth, their growth, their growing old and their death; they will now be able to recognise more easily the progress of her second birth and of that very perfection whereto she has risen again in our times.

Source C: Leonardo da Vinci's notebook.

I am fully aware that the fact of my not being a man of letters may cause certain arrogant persons to think that they may with reason censure me, alleging that I am a man ignorant of book-learning. Foolish folk! Do they not know that I might retort, as did Marius to the Roman patricians, 'They who themselves go about adorned in the labour of others will not permit me of my own' . . . The Painter will produce pictures of little merit if he takes the works of others as his standard; but if he will apply himself to learn from the objects of nature, he will produce good results. This we see was the case with the painters who came after the time of the Romans, for they continually imitated each other, and from age to age their art steadily declined.

Source D: Girolamo Savonarola, 1494.

You painters do an ill thing; if you knew what I know and the scandal it produces, you would not paint them . . . do you believe the Virgin Mary went dressed this way, as you paint her? I tell you she went dressed as a poor woman, simply and so covered that her face could hardly be seen, and likewise St Elizabeth went dressed simply. You would do well to obliterate these figures that are painted so unchastely. You make the Virgin Mary seem dressed like a whore.

Source E: Baldassare Castiglione to Pope Leo X, 1513.

How much lime has been burned from the statues and ornaments of ancient time? I am bold to ask how much of all this new Rome that we see today, however great, however beautiful, however adorned with palaces and churches and the buildings, has been built of lime made from ancient marbles?

Questions

1. What does Baldassare Castiglione (Source E) mean by 'this new Rome'? (2)
2. Express in your own words the arguments by which Leonardo (Source C) rejects the need for an artist to have a classical education. (3)
*3. On what grounds does Vasari (Sources A and B) claim contemporary developments as both a 'new birth' and a 're-birth'? How convincing do you find his conclusions? (5)
4. What objections to the contemporary developments in art are expressed by the writers of these sources? (6)
5. Using these sources and your own knowledge, discuss how much was new and how much 'reborn' about the art of the Renaissance. (9)

Worked answer

*2. [It is essential to get all you can out of the two sources, and still leave yourself enough time to express your own views.]

Source A identifies two influences from classical times. Firstly, the 'Greek' sculptors employed at the cathedral in Pisa, who may well have been from South Italy, but who were perceived as being heirs to the inheritance of the classical age; and secondly, the example of the genuine classical works, brought back by the Pisan fleet on its return from trading activities in the Eastern Mediterranean. Such collection of artistic and literary 'loot' was a feature of fifteenth-century trade, and was certainly influential in shaping the Renaissance. In Source B Vasari specifically talks about a second birth, and the 'very perfection' of his age, as something previously unknown. He does, however, clearly also regard the development of art as cyclical, since it has 'risen again'. The use of a human metaphor is in itself a very 'Renaissance' approach to the issue. Artists at the time saw themselves both as learning from the ancients and as developing new techniques and ideas unknown in classical times, and these two sources taken together reflect that. Without the classical inspiration, Renaissance art might have developed very differently; at the same time, the new and unique features of Renaissance art are equally significant.

SOURCES

2. HUMANISM AND THE RICH

Source F: Vittorino da Feltre (d.1446) explains his ideas on education.

We call those studies 'liberal' which are worthy of a free man; those studies by which we attain and practise virtue and wisdom; that education which calls forth, trains and develops those highest gifts of body and mind which ennoble men and which are rightly judged to rank next in dignity to virtue alone. For to a vulgar temper, gain and pleasure are the sole aims of existence, to a lofty nature, moral work and fame.

Source G: Carlo Masuppini, 1446.

There can be no doubt, I think, about how highly the art of music was esteemed by the ancients, who far excel all others in wisdom. To begin with the philosophers, we find that Pythagoras and those who listened to him thought the

study of music so important, that they attributed separate sirens to every sphere ... Plato, that wise and almost divine man ... believed that if you change the music you change the ethos of the city. Take Aristotle, who thought the art of music was necessary for the good life.

Source H: Nicolas Copernicus to Bishop Lucas Watzelrode, 1509.

I deemed it inequitable for the Epistles of Theophylactus to be read only in the Greek language. To make them more generally accessible, I have tried to translate them into Latin, to the best of my ability.

Source I: Thomas More to the council of Oxford University.

To whom is it not obvious that to the Greeks we owe all our precision in the liberal arts generally and in theology particularly, for the Greeks either made the great discoveries themselves or passed them on as part of their heritage. Take philosophy, for example. If you leave out Cicero and Seneca, the Romans wrote their philosophy in Greek or translated it from Greek.

Source J: Guillaume Budé to Pierre Lamy, 1523.

I learn that you and Rabelais ... because of your zeal in the study of the Greek tongue, are harassed and vexed in a thousand ways by your brothers, those sworn enemies of all literature and all refinement. O fatal madness! O incredible error! Thus the gross and stupid monks have been so carried away by their blindness as to pursue with calumnies those whose learning ... should be an honour to the entire community.

Questions

1. Explain what is meant by 'vulgar temper' (Source F) and 'sirens' (Source G). (2)
2. How 'generally accessible' (Source H) do you think that Theophylactus would become if translated into Latin? (3)
3. Sources I and J both confront the fact that some groups were opposed to the study of Greek. Which do you find the more convincing as an argument in favour of the study of Greek? (5)
*4. What evidence can you find in these sources that knowledge of Greek was an essential qualification for an educated man of the Renaissance? (7)
5. To what extent do these sources suggest that the content of Renaissance education was only appropriate to the members of the 'ruling classes'? Does your other knowledge support the conclusion you have reached? (8)

Worked answer

*4. [Make sure that you consider every source in turn, while at the same time avoiding using information which you may have used in other answers.]

While Source F does not specifically mention the study of Greek, nevertheless, it is describing the kind of education perceived as essential to enable humans to achieve their highest potential, so the fact that Greek is not specifically mentioned may well be seen as arguing against the premise of the question. Source G, on the other hand, uses the Greeks as the main reason why music should be studied. The citing of Pythagoras, Plato and Aristotle shows that the writer is aiming to imitate the supreme minds of ancient Greece. Copernicus, in Source H, appears to suggest that the inability to read Greek does handicap would-be scholars; thus he offers a translation to make the work in question more accessible. He accepts that not everyone who wants to be educated can learn and use Greek, and thus translation is essential. Source I suggests that all philosophy and theology is based in Greek and thus knowledge of Greek is essential for academic study. And finally, Source J makes clear that the study of Greek can bring honour on a whole community, and thus those who oppose it have no right to do so, and are in error. Taken together, these sources indicate that the ability to read Greek was an asset to the educated man during the Renaissance. But it was not essential: translations existed; and the ideas of the Greeks were already informing all aspects of intellectual life.

3

THE INFLUENCE OF THE RENAISSANCE ON MONARCHIES AND GOVERNMENTS

BACKGROUND NARRATIVE

During the fifteenth and sixteenth centuries, the nature of government changed in many parts of Europe. It has been suggested that these changes are closely linked with the Renaissance, and that 'the Renaissance witnessed a widespread rise of nationalism, which undermined both the feudal system and the concept of a Holy Roman Empire'. (1)

Government in the Middle Ages had been based on the personal holdings and inheritance of the royal and noble families. England had held large areas of France through inheritance and marriage, for example, under Henry II, rather than conquest. Loyalty was supposed to be due to the feudal overlord, regardless of his nationality, so that in large areas of Central Europe, regions of varying language and culture recognised the overlordship of the Holy Roman Emperor. Wars were fought making use of the feudal obligation to support the overlord in conflict, from the 'host' made up of unskilled peasants to the trained knights who held their fiefdoms on condition that they fought when called upon to do so. In theory, kings were chosen by God and so the Church wielded substantial influence over governments and dynasties.

During the fifteenth and sixteenth centuries government took new shapes, and new attitudes emerged, the rulers more powerful and the nobles less, and these changes have been associated with the Renaissance. Writings about the theory of government, such as those of Machiavelli, were numerous and widely discussed, with classical sources being translated and referred to. States became recognisably more 'national', and more defined by geographical borders: England, for example, lost the last of her holdings in France by the middle of the sixteenth century. The last non-Christian holding on the Iberian Peninsula was lost in 1492; despite attempts to gain land in Italy, France's southern borders became recognisably those of the Alps and Pyrenees. Switzerland defined itself as a nation, with its own heroes and identity; and by the beginning of the seventeenth century similar nationalist aspirations were realised in the Netherlands.

The forms of government which developed in this period tended to focus power in the hands of the monarch at the expense of other classes and groups. In almost all the countries of Europe, the tradition of seeking advice and approval from representatives of the people assembled in Cortes, Diet or Estates declined. Neither in Castile nor in France did the tradition of summoning town as well as noble and clergy representatives survive the sixteenth century. The French Estates General met in 1484, 1560, 1614 and then not again until 1789! In Spain taxation was possible without reference to the Castilian Cortes, and while that of Aragon maintained its rights, it was increasingly bypassed. Only in England did Parliament grow in influence rather than declining, possibly because King Henry VIII needed an outward show of popular support when he decided to risk alienating all of Catholic Christendom. It seems possible that the personification of national pride in the King himself was a development of nationalist feeling.

National pride was appealed to, for example by Joan of Arc in her war against English control in France, in the attack by Ferdinand and Isabella upon Granada, and in Scottish resistance to English claims. Awareness of city identity in Italy began to be transformed into awareness of Italian interests, under the threat of foreign attack from France, at least for readers of Guiccardini's *Storia d'Italia* (1534–40). Machiavelli ended *The Prince* with a plea for the unification of Italy.

Rulers were prepared to spend money on enhancing their own status in all kinds of ways, and the new developments in the arts gave them every opportunity. Formal court ceremonial was matched by sumptuous clothing and embellishment to demonstrate the status of the monarch. The portraits of rulers, such as those of Henry VIII by Holbein, Francis I by Titian, or the Medici by Gozzoli or Raphael, reveal their wealth in fabric, jewels and furnishing. They built fine palaces and surrounded themselves with the best musicians and scholars.

Technical developments meant that war became a skilled occupation. Until the fourteenth century, rulers had made use of the 'host': peasants could be required to fight under their lords' commands for forty days. Now, however, such reluctant amateurs were no longer adequate to handle the new weapons, and thus rulers had begun to employ mercenaries to fight their wars for them. Skilled troops were a valuable resource, and such forces could earn considerable income for their leaders. The popes, at the heart of the warring Italian states, began to recruit their guards from Switzerland, as they still do today. By the end of the fifteenth century, however, loyalty purchased by the employer was being regarded as unreliable. Machiavelli pointed out that the main concern was to survive to fight again, and that troops could be persuaded to change sides by the simple offer of a better deal. The development of standing armies was bound to follow, although no European monarch extended the concept of permanent loyalty as far as the Ottoman emperors with their Janissaries.

The rulers of this period, as indeed in any period, were prepared to use any method to advance the needs of their own territories. Formal diplomacy developed with the placing of permanent ambassadors, who wrote daily dispatches home to their masters. Ceremonial meetings, such as that at the Field of Cloth of Gold, near Calais (1520), were prepared for by months of detailed negotiation by a new breed of professional diplomats. Treaties became increasingly complex as attempts were made to safeguard lands, titles and future commitments. Such agreements were not, however, necessarily kept. Alliances changed, and promises were broken when advantage seemed to point in a new direction: as, for example, when Ferdinand of Aragon persuaded the Emperor Maximilian to

Plate 4 North-west façade of the Château at Chambord, France.
Photo © Lonchampt, Arch.Phot.Paris/SPADEM,
© C.N.M.H.S./SPADEM

make peace with France without bothering to inform his son-in-law and ally Henry VIII of his intentions (1513).

Although monarchs of the period continued to insist that their position and powers were God-given, they were disinclined to accept the full authority of God's representative on earth, the pope. These doubts date back to the fourteenth-century Avignon period, when the papacy acted in accordance with French foreign policy, and were never dispelled. In Italy, rulers of the city states did not hesitate to fight against Rome if their territorial ambitions demanded this. Further afield, the issue of who controlled the considerable wealth and influence of the Church led to changes in the historic relationships between pope and state. Only in England was there a complete schism. But in France control of the day-to-day running of the Church was transferred to the monarch by the Concordat of 1516; and the Gallican Church was as much under the control of the king of France as England's Church was under its king. In Spain the Catholic monarchs established that they, and not the pope, should have the right of provision to dioceses in Castile's new holdings abroad. The Avis kings of Portugal controlled the Order of Christ and thus all the missionaries of their worldwide empire.

Fifteenth- and sixteenth-century governments were different from those of the Middle Ages, and historians in the past have linked these changes directly to the Renaissance. (2) Many of the trends which are associated with this period can, however, be discerned in earlier years; and throughout the Renaissance period motives, methods and outcomes which might be said to be 'medieval' continued to exist. Nevertheless, the fact that the label is attached to government suggests that it is worth considering whether there were monarchs who particularly fitted the title of 'Renaissance prince' and whether there were distinctively nationalist developments in this period. The two analyses which follow focus on these points.

ANALYSIS (1): IS THE TITLE 'PRINCE OF THE RENAISSANCE' AN APPROPRIATE ONE FOR ANY MONARCH?

Many of the monarchs of the period were aware of living in an exciting time, and of doing things in a new way. Books about government were written for them and read by them. Kings felt that their heirs should be taught how to govern, and employed scholars with a wealth of classical examples of good and bad government, as tutors. This was also a period of ostentation, when Manuel of Portugal, who did not keep a glorious court and whose clothes were said to be mildewed and motheaten, was ridiculed for his meanness. Rulers appointed court musicians and painters, and took an interest in geography and zoology; they were prepared to challenge long-held views and the papal authority which had, in the Middle Ages, been paramount. For the purposes of this chapter, we shall consider three rulers who each have claims to be thought of predominantly as Renaissance figures.

Charles V, Holy Roman Emperor, appears at first an unlikely candidate to be perceived as a Renaissance prince, since his title and status were medieval rather than modern. The feudal Holy Roman Empire was already breaking up, and Charles did his best to hold it together. His widespread inheritance was the result of feudal and dynastic traditions, deriving in part from the marriages of his grand-parents. The Habsburg claim to Hungary was that of overlord. And yet Charles behaved in many ways as a typical Renaissance ruler should. He approached the issues which confronted him with intelligence and a commitment to justice. His widespread empire meant that he had to become something of a linguist, and he was interested in art and in music. He was reluctant to condemn Luther without a hearing, and gave him safe conduct to and from the meeting at Worms in 1521. He felt the abuses of the Church needed to be confronted, and it was his pressure which resulted in the summoning of the Council of Trent (1545), very much against the wishes of the Vatican, which recalled the damaging years of the fourteenth- and fifteenth-century conciliar movement. But some of his religious policies were far from 'modern'. Like his medieval ancestors, he longed to crusade against the Muslims, and launched expensive attacks against North Africa. He endorsed the work of the Inquisition, which may be said to be the antithesis of the questioning and enquiring spirit of the Renaissance.

He was never able to conduct his foreign policies in Europe in the chivalric way he admired from his reading. Shortage of money led to a range of compromises, and he deplored the bad faith of others, notably the King of France. The failure of Francis I to ransom his sons after the Treaty of Madrid (1526) shocked him, and the boys were released in 1529 without the fulfilment of the treaty obligations by their father.

As ruler of Spain, he encouraged the establishment of new univer-sities and the publication of academic works. With the expansion of the Spanish Empire in America, Charles himself was most concerned for the well-being of the native American peoples. He listened to the lectures of Vitoria on the subject of the ethics of conquest, and offered personal support to Bartolomé de las Casas, one of the few to champion the rights of the natives. But it could be argued that this attitude was mainly designed to prevent the establishment of a wealthy and autonomous conquistador class in the New World, and thus was merely a sensible approach rather than a sign of particular enlightenment. In the Low Countries, where he felt most at home although he spent more time in Spain than there, it has been suggested that he failed to notice the development of nationalist feelings which were to culminate in the independence of the Netherlands at the start of the seventeenth century.

Although Charles was interested in the developments of the Renaissance, he did not adopt new or distinctive forms of government. Indeed, as J.H. Elliot demonstrates, (3) Charles rejected suggestions that he might centralise his diffuse empire or establish mechanisms which would increase the efficiency of government, preferring to rule each part in a way which, as closely as possible, matched its own traditions and maintained his personal connections. If Charles had had his way, it seems probable that traditional forms of government would have continued throughout his lifetime.

Charles's lifetime rival, Francis I of France, is often considered a prince of the Renaissance because he ruled France during the years when its culture flourished very strongly, and because he played such an important part in this cultural flowering. He bought paintings and sculptures from Italy. It was he who brought Leonardo da Vinci to France, where he spent the last years of his life. Benevenuto Cellini was also enticed to France by generous offers from Francis. The porcelain works at Limoges and the tapestry factory at Fontainebleau benefited from his patronage. Francis presided over the building of some of the most beautiful chateaux of the Renaissance period, including Chambord in the Loire Valley. His court was the most sumptuous of its time in Europe, both as regards clothes and furnishings and in terms of ceremonial and formality. If a Renaissance ruler were to be defined purely in terms of appearance, Francis epitomises the role.

At the same time, it was Francis who centralised the government and institutions of France, building on the work of Louis XI, and thus laying the foundations of absolute monarchy. He pushed France in a new direction, with the guidance of Budé and de Seyssel. The Estates General did not meet once in his reign; Francis preferred to use nobles whose loyalty he could ensure by the judicious provision of pensions, lands and other privileges. He employed a mixture of clergy and laymen, but then so had his predecessors. Despite being sympathetic to Reformation ideas, Francis recognised the need to maintain the cohesive force of a single Church, particularly since he had ensured royal control of the Church through the 1516 Concordat of Bologna. Reformist ideas made little headway in France, although where there were conversions to Protestantism, these were determined enough to survive the persecution of later reigns.

Francis was not particularly successful in his foreign policy, and yet here he was not prepared to compromise. It could be argued that his aims were truly those of a Renaissance prince: geographical integrity for his borders, and glory for his nation. The costs to his people were excessive, however. Despite the fact that France had the opportunity of peace after a century of war against England, Francis's predecessors had gone to war in Italy, and Francis adopted this policy with enthusiasm, fighting wars against the Habsburg powers in Spain and the Holy Roman Empire for almost all of his reign. Truces and treaties were signed from time to time, but the wars went on, even after Francis was captured at Pavia (1525). The fact that, having exchanged himself for his two young sons, he then failed to fulfil the treaty obligations which would release them damaged his reputation then and indeed has since, particularly since he did not reduce his own extravagance even when taxing his people heavily to raise the necessary 2 million ecus-au-soleil, said to amount to more than four and a half tons of gold. (4)

Henry VIII of England was certainly a Renaissance individual. 'He is very accomplished,' wrote the Venetian Ambassador in 1519, 'a good musician, composes well, is a most capital horseman, a fine jouster, speaks good French, Latin and Spanish'. (5) He was friendly with scholars, such as Thomas More, and felt that the right way to counteract the ideas of Luther was by himself publishing a paper asserting the veracity of the Seven Sacraments. His children were even better educated than he had been, each of the three being renowned throughout Europe for their learning. He employed painters of the quality of Holbein, and he continued his father's palace-building programme.

As a ruler, Henry was strong-willed in the way that Machiavelli had said was essential if a prince was to do what was best for his country. He selected ministers who would be loyal to him, and disposed of them callously when they failed to do his bidding, as he did with Wolsey. The needs, as he perceived them, of the government came before any sentiment about long and faithful service. He dealt ruthlessly with those who opposed him, and those who appeared to be a threat to him, like the few remaining Yorkists. (In 1541 he ordered the execution of the seventy-two-year-old Countess of Salisbury.) But kings throughout the Middle Ages had been capable of ruthlessness. He did not hesitate to go to war when it seemed sensible, for example, in supporting the Holy League against France; but equally, he would reverse his alliances if he felt it was wise to do so, as he did when he annulled his marriage to the Princess of Cleves, which, it seemed to him, put him too firmly into the Protestant camp in the struggles in Germany.

Henry was not afraid to take decisions which were radical and contained an element of risk. His break with Rome was not, however, based upon Renaissance study of the Bible, but upon his own determination to have his own way. There was nothing particularly advanced in resisting the pope: after all, King John, in the early thirteenth century, had allowed England to be interdicted for twelve years, rather than give in to the pope. But Henry was able to carry his people with him, and did not face the kind of civil strife which had eventually forced John to give in. The success of the Henrician Reformation, rather than the fact that it was attempted, may be the clearest proof of changes in popular attitudes, and of a growing sense of Englishness.

Henry's long reign (thirty-eight years) saw many changes, social, economic and political as well as religious. If a pragmatic approach to problems as they arose may be taken as a Renaissance approach, then it would be reasonable to call Henry a 'Renaissance prince'. But it may be more accurate to say that he simply followed in his father's footsteps and ruled in the way his people expected.

Henry VIII followed his father's policies, and maintained the security of his realm without embarking on radically new policies: even in religion, he was conservative except over the issue of the Supremacy of Rome. Charles V's rule, too, looked back as much as it looked forward, using the forms and the ideals of previous ages. Of the three monarchs that have been considered, Francis I probably comes closest to being a true Renaissance prince. During his reign, the arts in France flourished as never before, and the nation itself was set upon the course which it was to pursue until the end of the eighteenth century.

Questions

1. What features do the reigns of the three monarchs considered here have in common? Are these typical 'Renaissance' features?
2. Choose a different ruler of the period and consider whether he might be considered a 'Renaissance prince'.

ANALYSIS (2): TO WHAT EXTENT IS IT POSSIBLE TO IDENTIFY A SPIRIT OF 'NATIONALISM' IN RENAISSANCE EUROPE?

During the fifteenth and sixteenth centuries, the city states of Europe began to move towards the forms and borders which were to last until the twenty-first century. Britain ceased to be a landholder on the continent of Europe. Spain, Portugal and France became distinct nations. On the other hand, many regions were to wait until the nineteenth or even twentieth century to achieve anything resembling autonomy: the states of Germany were separate except for the tenuous and medieval link of the Holy Roman Empire; Italy was a geographical area, but not a political entity; the south-eastern areas of Europe were in the possession of the Turks, and in the north-east, Poland–Lithuania and the Baltic states were barely beginning to achieve identities; the Scandinavian countries did not attain separate nationhoods until the early twentieth century.

Whatever the borders, however, the peoples of Europe appear to have become more nationalistic during the period of the Renaissance. The increased use of the vernacular in business served to strengthen the identity of each nation while speeding the process by which they became alienated from each other. In England and Scotland vernacular writers such as Elyot and Starkey favoured their own land, 'my natural country' (6), over those of foreigners, and in 1539 Richard Moryson wrote 'let us fight this one field with English hands and English hearts'. (7) English playwrights and poets from Skelton (?1460–1529) onwards made a point of ridiculing the strange habits of foreigners. Xenophobia was a durable and popular English trait. Charles V warned his son about the notorious attitudes of the English towards foreigners when Philip was on his way to England to marry Mary Tudor (1554). The same feelings can be found expressed in the fourteenth century, in hostility towards the merchants of the Hanseatic League. At the same time, local rather than national loyalties remained strong, showing themselves particularly when the central government attempted to impose unwanted policies or taxes. Examples are the tax rebellions in Cornwall against Henry VII and the religious Pilgrimage of Grace in Yorkshire and Lincolnshire during Henry VIII's reign. These risings were as much expressions of local grievances as any during the Middle Ages. In France, the attempt to take over areas such as Brittany and Burgundy, however logical in geographical terms, were resisted by all the inhabitants and not just by the nobles whose power bases were threatened. Nationalism perhaps applied to these smaller areas, but this was not a new feeling.

In Spain, the union, through the marriage of Ferdinand and Isabella, of Castile and Aragon was accompanied by statements like that of the Cortes of Aragon, 'we are all brothers now', and policies were favoured which were supposed to be for the good of the whole peninsula, for example, concerning currency and trade. On the other hand, the kingdoms of Spain continued to be governed separately, even when Emperor Charles V inherited the lands of both his grandparents. The voyages of exploration, and the resulting empire, were the concern of Castile exclusively; on the occasions when Aragonese involvement was permitted, great emphasis was placed on the exceptional nature of the permission.

The same pattern can be seen in all the countries of Europe. Where it seemed useful, appeal was made to national feeling as, for example, when Luther remarked 'we Germans cannot attend St Peter's'; (8) but the Holy Roman Emperor continued to claim jurisdiction over cities such as Milan, and France claimed areas which were, by language and inclination, Italian. National status was cited as a reason for breaking treaty obligations or for ostentation at international events like royal betrothal ceremonies, and yet this kind of behaviour is as old as international relations themselves.

It has been suggested, for example, by Antony Maczak (9) that feelings of nationalism were newly developed, and were the province of the élite, just as the experience of Renaissance culture and art in areas such as Poland was confined to rich and noble patrons. Indeed, in Poland, the nobles who controlled the choice of monarch regularly elected foreign rulers, specifically to prevent the development of a strong and centralised government which might reduce their influence. To limit nationalism to the educated classes is, however, to ignore attitudes and feelings which were changing during this period. Loyalties which had tied the common people to their lord or to their area were now attached more to the nation and to the success and glory of the monarch who epitomised it.

Questions

1. Did changes in warfare, and in the technology of travel, encourage or discourage the development of feelings of nationhood in Europe?
2. Why do you think large areas of Europe maintained feudal and non-national structures for so long?

SOURCES

1. RENAISSANCE PERCEPTIONS OF GOOD AND BAD GOVERNMENT

Source A: Erasmus to Henry VIII 1517.

. . . moreover, as an intelligent and pious prince is wise, vigilant and provident for the whole community, being one that is transacting not his own business but that of the public, so it is right, that every man should endeavour to the utmost of his power to help him in his cares and anxieties; and the wider his empire, the more need has he of this kind of service. A sovereign is an exceptional being among mortals, an image of the Deity; and yet he is a man.

Source B: Luther discusses the power of the civil authority over faith, 1522.

A judge should and must be very certain in giving judgement and have everything before him in clear light. But the thoughts and meanings of the soul can be clear to none but God. Therefore it is futile and impossible to command or to force any man to believe this or that . . . Thus is it each man's business what he believes; and he himself must see to it that he believe aright. As little as another can go to heaven or hell for me, as little as he can shut or open to me heaven or hell, so little can he compel me to believe or disbelieve.

Source C: John Calvin on the rights of princes, 1541.

Wherefore, if we are cruelly vexed by an inhuman Prince, or robbed and plundered by one prodigal or avaricious, or despised and left without protection by one negligent; or even if we are afflicted for the Name of God by one sacrilegious and unbelieving, let us first of all remember those our own offences against God which doubtless are chastised by these plagues. And secondly, let us consider that it is not for us to remedy those evils; for us it remains only to implore the aid of God, in whose hands are the hearts of Kings and changes of Kingdoms.

Source D: Savonarola attacks Lorenzo de' Medici, 1490.

The tyrant is wont to busy his people with spectacles and festivities, that they may think of their pastimes and not of his designs, and becoming unaccustomed to the conduct of the commonwealth, leave the reins of government in his hands . . . Tyrants are incorrigible because they are proud, because they love flattery, because they will not restore their ill-gotten gains. They allow bad officials to have their way; they yield to adulation; they neither heed the poor nor condemn the rich . . . The people are oppressed by taxes, and when they come to pay unbearable sums, the rich cry: 'Give me the rest' . . . when widows come weeping, they are told, 'go to sleep'. When the poor complain, they are told, 'pay, pay'.

Source E: Machiavelli's obituary on Lorenzo de' Medici (d.1492).

Of fortune and of God he was supremely loved, wherefore all his enterprises ended well and those of his enemies ill . . . All the citizens mourned his death and all the princes of Italy . . . and that they had good reason to grieve the result soon showed . . . as soon as Lorenzo died, all those bad seeds began to sprout which not long after, he who could quell them being no longer alive, ruined and are still ruining Italy

Questions

1. Explain why Erasmus (Source A) might have had a special interest in the behaviour and attitudes of Henry VIII. (2)
2. For what reasons does Calvin (Source C) insist on obedience to the civil authority? To what extent is this teaching supported by the Christian scriptures? (4)
*3. Compare the views of Lorenzo de' Medici expressed in Sources D and E. To what extent is it possible to reconcile these two contrasting views? (5)
4. What is the basis of princely authority according to *each* of these sources? (6)
5. Using these sources and your own knowledge, discuss the extent to which there was agreement in the Renaissance on the nature of good monarchy. (8)

Worked answer

*3. Savonarola condemns tyrants like Lorenzo for being proud and refusing to share his power: he looks back, by implication, to the time when Florence was not run by one man alone; Machiavelli, on the other hand, appears to approve of his authority, since his death meant that evil developments were unchecked. While Savonarola emphasises his grasping taxation and derides the way revenues were spent on spectacles and festivities, Machiavelli merely claims that fortune smiled on Lorenzo so that all went well. Savonarola states that he appointed bad officials, while Machiavelli focuses on Lorenzo's own rule. Above all, Savonarola describes someone who was hated, while Machiavelli describes someone who was loved. These contrasting views can be seen as two sides of the same character; Machiavelli believed firm government was essential in times of crisis, and argued elsewhere that citizens must pay for protection from their enemies, both in loss of freedom and in taxation. Savonarola was hostile to all authority except God's, and antagonised the Church as much as he did the secular rulers whom he attacked.

SOURCES

2. EXAMPLES OF THEORY AND PRACTICE OF GOVERNMENT IN THE RENAISSANCE

Source F: Machiavelli in *The Discorsi* I xi.

When one of the parties begins to favour a single individual, tyranny soon arises ... And when a *popolo* [popular group] makes the mistake of building a man's prestige to help him oppose those whom it hates, if he is clever, he is sure to become Tyrant of the City.

Source G: Francesco Guicciardini (1483–1540) discusses Tacitus.

If you want to know what the thoughts of tyrants are, read in Cornelius Tacitus the last conversations of the dying Augustus with Tiberius. Cornelius Tacitus teaches those who live under tyrants how to live and act prudently; just as he teaches tyrants ways to secure their powers.

Source H: The Duke of Mantua explains why he is glad to have a drawing by Mantegna.

... frequently ambassadors and lords come, and to honour them one seeks to show them stupendous works, and I will now have this marvellous drawing to show.

Source I: Leonardo da Vinci to Ludovico Sforza, Duke of Milan, ?1482.

1. I can construct bridges which are very light and strong and very portable with which to pursue and defeat the enemy; and others more solid which resist fire or assault yet are easily removed and placed in position; and I can also burn and destroy those of the enemy.
2. In case of a siege I can cut off water from the trenches and make pontoons and scaling ladders and other similar contrivances.

3. If by reason of the elevation or the strength of its position a place cannot be bombarded, I can demolish every fortress if its foundations have not been set in stone.
4. I can also make a kind of cannon which is light and easy of transport with which to hurl small stones like hail and of which the smoke causes great terror to the enemy, so that they suffer heavy loss and confusion.
5. I can noiselessly construct to any prescribed point subterranean passages, either straight or curving, passing if necessary underneath trenches or a river.

Questions

1. How convincing do you find the Duke of Mantua's reasons (Source H) for wanting to possess works of art? What other reasons might he have had? (3)
2. Explain briefly who are the people referred to in Source G. What does Guicciardini's reference to them tell us about political theory in the Renaissance period? (4)
3. By comparing Sources F and G, discuss the extent to which the concept of 'tyranny' was a negative one in this period. (4)
*4. Study Source I. What can be learned about the nature of Renaissance warfare from this letter? (6)
5. Considering each of these sources in turn and using your own knowledge of the period, discuss whether they are accurate reflections of the ways in which rulers governed during the Renaissance. (8)

Worked answer

*4. [Make sure that you show your own knowledge of the period by introducing supportive details to back up what you are finding in the source.]

First, it is clear that rulers were willing to hire expertise in war from whatever source it came: Leonardo, himself a Florentine, was looking for employment in Milan. The use of mercenaries was a growing trend in this period. Renaissance warfare, at least in Italy, was clearly a matter of sieges: three of Leonardo's claims are to do with besieging fortresses, demolishing them and gaining access by tunnelling. At the same time rapid pursuit could be a priority, and the particular problems of the Italian terrain, with its many rivers, are important considerations when attack or retreat are being planned. New technology and the improvement of cannon (at this stage just over 100 years old in Europe) are also matters of importance. The letter does not, however, dwell on the new developments in the building of fortifications, in which Leonardo was also said to be very skilled.

4

THE LINKS BETWEEN THE RENAISSANCE AND THE REFORMATION

BACKGROUND NARRATIVE

When one intellectual movement follows and overlaps chrono-logically with another, it is inevitable that links will be sought, and probably found between them. This is particularly true of the Reformation, as historians seek to understand the reasons why the sixteenth-century Reformation succeeded in permanently splitting the Church in Western Europe, where all previous disputes had failed to do so.

Heresy was not new. Throughout its history, the Church had been threatened by theological views which differed from its teachings. Indeed, one such dispute, in 1054, had resulted in the separate development of the Eastern (Orthodox) Church. Since then, however, the Roman Church had maintained its supremacy in the face of many heretical movements. The most recent were at the end of the fourteenth century, when the Bohemian John Huss and the English John Wyclif preached views which attacked the position of the pope. They argued against the wealth of the Church, and hoped to make the scriptures accessible to all. In theology, they denied the special status of the clergy and above all the pope, a doctrine which Luther was to formalise as 'the priesthood of all believers'. The failure of their movements is interesting because some of their ideas were similar to those which would be put forward by Martin Luther. Why did he succeed when they had failed?

One reason may be that the humanists of the fifteenth century had made criticism of the clergy acceptable. At the same time, they encouraged accurate textual study of the Bible. Erasmus did not break with the Roman Church; but the climate created by his writings, and those of scholars such as Valla, provided the environment in which Luther's writings were accepted. The issue of the abuses in the Church was one of the topics which was raised by the humanists. But the Vatican's need for money was in its turn partly a result of the Renaissance. Rivalry in Italy, both military and political, and the competitive patronage of the great artists, ensured that the great Renaissance popes would squeeze all the revenue they could from the faithful. The way in which the popes embellished their palaces and churches with pagan themes also encouraged doubts in their genuine Christianity, and fears of a reborn paganism, as suggested by Erasmus in 1517. (1)

The Church had always put forward the doctrine of authority: namely, that the great fathers of the Church had, over time, been granted additional insights into the truth of the Bible and God's workings. The mid-fourteenth century and the Black Death saw a reduction in the popular acceptance of this doctrine and the suggestion, for example, by Wyclif, that the behaviour of the Church fathers was actually angering God. The Church had been unable to provide convincing explanations for the disaster of the plague and, while it had been happy to blame minority groups for spreading the disease, it could not explain why God had allowed even the virtuous to suffer so terribly. The Renaissance discoveries in science and geography, which so patently contradicted both the Bible and the teachings of the Church, had the effect of further weakening papal and clerical authority, until it was no longer axiomatic that the pope and the Church were the sources of all truth.

Into this atmosphere of questioning and doubt stepped Martin Luther (1483–1546), with a protest which began over indulgences and money raised for St Peter's Basilica in Rome, but soon expanded to embrace the Supremacy of Rome, the meaning of the Eucharist and the issue of whether good works were needed for salvation. His first protest, the 95 Theses of 1517, was followed by a substantial number of writings, almost all in the vernacular, and all spread, unlike the ideas of Huss and Wyclif, by the power of the printing press. Luther's thorough, humanist-style study of the Epistle to the Romans had demonstrated to his satisfaction that justification (or salvation) was by faith alone. (2) The other great reformers, Ulrich Zwingli (1484–1531) and John Calvin (1509–1564), extended Luther's intellectual arguments. Zwingli, for example, denied the possibility of the real presence at the Eucharist, following long study of the words spoken by Jesus as quoted in three of the Gospels. (3) This kind of scholarly research, as opposed to acceptance of the Church's teaching, may be said to be typical of the Renaissance. Calvin's extension of the doctrine of justification by faith to mean predestination was also rooted firmly in biblical scholarship. (4)

By the time of Calvin's death, Europe had ceased to be a religious unity. Some states, for example, England, had become officially 'Protestant', while in others religion was fought over for years, as in France, or divided area and class, as in Scotland. Switzerland was one of the few areas where compromise was reached, with some whole cantons accepting the reformist teachings while others remained Catholic. The Holy Roman Emperor had been forced to accept that, within the states of Germany at least, each ruler should decide, a decision enshrined in the Augsburg Statement of 1555, 'cuius regio, eius religio'. While some parts of Europe, notably Southern Italy and Spain, remained Catholic, the authorities had to be endlessly vigilant, and constructed institutions to prevent the spread of the virus of Protestantism.

These institutions, known collectively as the Counter-Reformation, or Catholic Reformation, have in themselves clear traces of Renaissance thinking. Even the Papal Index of prohibited books, at first sight a totally reactionary piece of repression, could be said to indicate the Vatican's recognition of the power of books and the strength of the printing press. The Inquisition was not new. In Spain it was cruel, and even in Italy its threat was to be enough to cause Galileo to recant. It may appear anti-intellectual, but it, like Luther's protest, had its basis in the teachings of Christ. (5) The Council of Trent (1545–63), which met at the persistent urging of Charles V, was designed to find, by discussion and debate, the solutions to the great problems which faced the Church, rather than relying on the authority of the pope alone to deal with them. Of the new religious orders, the Society of Jesus, with its emphasis on intellectual rigour, and education, may be seen to reflect most directly the preoccupations of the Renaissance era.

Thus, while changes in the Church were long overdue, and had been presaged for more than a century, it was the Renaissance which provided both the intellectual and physical means by which the changes were accomplished, both by reformist sects breaking away, and by the Roman Church addressing its own problems. If the printing press was crucial to the spread of the Reformation, (6) then so were the thought processes of the Renaissance, and the political context of the time. The two analyses which follow consider these aspects.

ANALYSIS (1): WAS MARTIN LUTHER 'A MAN OF THE RENAISSANCE'?

Luther's thinking was a mixture of the traditional and the modern. The stories which are told of his early life describe the kind of superstitions which are associated with the Middle Ages. Caught in a storm, he is supposed to have bargained aloud, 'St Anne, save me, I will be a monk.' For a man who was later to deny the value of the intercession of the saints, to make his plea to the grandmother of Christ is an indication of the extent to which he had absorbed and accepted the views of the medieval Church. Throughout his life he 'was quite willing to acknowledge that the devil could intervene in human affairs' (7) and wrote in 1530 to his friend Ludwig Senfl,

> For we know that music is also hateful and intolerable to the evil spirits. And I plainly judge, nor am I ashamed to assert, that there is no art, after theology, that can match music; for it alone, after theology, lends that which otherwise only theology lends, to wit, quiet and a contented mind. (8)

His scrupulous study of the Bible was very much in the new tradition of humanism. When confronted with a question he could not resolve, or a new idea, he tested it against the revealed word of God. It was this direct study of the Bible which led him to reject the sacrament of penance, a useful source of revenue for the Roman Church, since the Gospels say clearly (9) that repentance is essential and the Church had made use of a translation stating that 'penance' was necessary. On the other hand, his knowledge of scripture was also used to refute some of the new ideas of the Renaissance. His verdict on Copernicus, in 1530 is a good example: (10) 'This fool wishes to reverse the entire science of astronomy, but sacred scripture tells us that Joshua commanded the sun to stand still, not the earth.'

Once Luther's campaign became a political one, it demonstrated many of the new ideas of Renaissance rulers. His appeal to German nationalism was a powerful one, beginning with the 95 Theses themselves, and echoing through the rest of his writings. His view was that obedience to the ruler, as prescribed by Christ (11) was essential, and this strengthened his attack on Rome. His objection to St Peter's was mainly that it was not accessible to Germans. He was prepared to attack the authority of the pope, because it was not based in the scriptures: Jesus had said that Peter was to be the basis of the Church, not all Peter's successors as bishops of Rome. But Luther was no revolutionary. Where the authority was properly constituted, it was entitled to full obedience. Although it was his teachings which aroused the peasants of Germany in 1525, 'His adherence to the existing social order demanded condemnation of the very people he had so greatly influenced and espoused' (12), and he urged the rulers of Germany to destroy 'the murdering thieving hordes of the peasants'. (13)

Luther's conviction that he was right, so different from the doubts and uncertainties of his early life, meant that he was very reluctant to compromise, or to see the other side in any debate. As his Church began to be established, his approach to it was authoritarian, though never as much so as John Calvin's attitude to his Church in Geneva. Luther's breach with Zwingli came, as one might expect, over the interpretation of a passage of scripture; but unlike, for example, the later Church of England, Luther was not prepared to accept any vagueness over the issue of the Real Presence at communion. In his conviction of his own authority, he bears a strong resemblance to the hierarchy of the medieval Roman Church.

Luther was enthusiastic for the technical and concrete developments of the Renaissance, however. His espousal of the German language as a medium of communication did not involve a 'levelling down' of the intellectual content, or beauty of what he wrote. His tracts are closely argued and clearly written, and some of his hymns are recognised and studied for their poetry rather than for their theological content. Above all, Luther's Reformation was made by the printing press. As A.G. Dickens has said, 'Thanks to the press his case could also be accurately and swiftly presented to the mass of more or less literate citizens', (14) and these literate Germans had been prepared by the work of the humanists of the fifteenth century. But where they had, in the main, criticised the Church without suggesting solutions, Luther offered a cogent and attractive alternative. His decision to side with the rulers against the peasants is an indication of his awareness of political reality.

Luther built on the early developments of Renaissance humanism, and made use of some of the ideas of the Renaissance. But in his heart, it seems, he retained some of the 'medieval' feelings which had caused him to be so terrified of the wrath of God. In the reformer who condemned confession as unnecessary, it is still possible to discern the frightened monk whose exasperated confessor had once urged him to go out and commit some real sins before coming to confession. (15) Exactly the same dependence on authority which had led him to try all the superstitious remedies for sin during his trip to Rome now convinced him that scripture contained all the answers and thus was not to be questioned. He was not a liberal, open-minded man of the Renaissance, but a scholar for whom the new traditions of humanism and the new technology of the printing press were both available and crucial.

Questions

1. Were Renaissance developments the main reasons why Luther succeeded in splitting the Church where Huss and Wyclif had failed?
2. Compare the attitudes of Luther, Zwingli and Calvin to the ideas of the Renaissance.

ANALYSIS (2): THE REFORMATION AS A POLITICAL RATHER THAN A RELIGIOUS DEVELOPMENT

The period of the Renaissance saw a great deal of discussion and writing about government and politics. In all the countries of Europe, authors turned their attention to the issues of how to rule, whether as instruction (Machiavelli) or as fiction (Thomas More). It is therefore useful to consider the extent to which the Reformation, as well, was a political movement and not merely a matter of theology.

Matters of theology were, of course, important. Not only were the structures and methods of the Church attacked; doctrinal issues were also debated, and Renaissance scholars found that much of the Church's teaching was not directly based on scripture. The Supremacy of Rome was rejected, on the basis that Christ had merely given the leadership of the Church to Peter, and not to his successors as popes. Similarly, the lucrative veneration of the saints was declared to be no more than superstition; and this despite the fact that Luther's patron, Frederick the Wise, was an enthusiastic relic collector. As education spread, the availability of the Bible in the vernacular meant that there was increasing debate about the theories which underlay Christianity.

The rejection of the doctrine of transubstantiation had serious and secular implications for the whole hierarchy of the Church. If the bread and wine of communion did not change into the actual body and blood of Christ, then priests themselves were not miracle workers. They had no more direct links to God than any other believer, and could not offer absolution. All men could intercede directly with heaven. The reformist teaching of the priesthood of all believers damaged both the status and the revenues of the Catholic Church, as did the doctrine of salvation by faith alone. The clergy had relied on the income from good works, which was lost wherever the Reformers were listened to.

Of course, attacking the Church was a matter of politics as much as of religion. The Renaissance ideas which were encouraging princes to define and establish their own authorities were also bound to affect their attitudes to religion. In England, the King's marital wishes were put above his duty of obedience to the laws of the Church; in France, the King was able to increase his power over the clergy without an actual breach with Rome; and the same was true for Ferdinand and Isabella of Spain, as well as their successor, Charles. Indeed, these rulers controlled patronage and the allocation of benefices without any recourse to a breach with Rome. The issue of authority was as much to do with national and regal ambitions as with the Donation to Peter.

In Germany, politics and national rivalries were crucial. The German humanists of the previous years had begun to develop the arguments which Luther used with such force, and 'the German laity, stimulated by a generation of anti-Roman propaganda, took Luther's side'. (16) But there were more down-to-earth issues than that. When Tetzel was authorised to sell indulgences in 1516, Frederick, Elector of Saxony, was not prepared to allow them to enter his territory. His remarkable relic collection, including such treasures as some of the straw from the crib at Bethlehem, and a couple of the thorns from the crown of thorns, provided all the help out of Purgatory that his subjects could possibly need. Or so he thought. Tetzel's indulgences, however, were so powerful and so 'instant' that citizens of Saxony were actually crossing the river to buy them. Luther's attack was therefore the duty of a loyal subject, as well as the initiation of a theological debate.

In the years that followed, Germany fractured, with some states becoming Protestant, while others remained Catholic. In part, at least, this was the result of political considerations. Emperor Charles V was convinced that the Church needed reform, but at the last he remained loyal to the papacy, because he recognised that an attack on one source of authority could inspire an attack on another, his own. Princes who were anxious to assert their own authority at the expense of that of the Holy Roman Emperor's overlordship found an attack on the Church to be an effective mechanism. Competition between the states meant that some rulers in Germany (such as in Bavaria) found it advantageous to remain true Catholics and then crusade against their neighbours, using a new issue as a pretext to fight their old battles. In Italy, such a rivalry between states focused on economic and defence issues, with a little artistic rivalry, rather than on religion, and had perhaps been less destructive, as a result, than the wars of religion which were to tear Germany apart in the seventeenth century.

In addition, as Henry VIII demonstrated in England and Wales, economic and financial benefits might well accrue. By 1536, when the King declared monasticism to be wrong or unnecessary, the Church controlled at least one-sixth of English land. The exigencies of his foreign policy meant that Henry was unable to keep hold of much of the land he had confiscated; but the fortunes and social status of many families were secured by the grant or purchase of such land, thus ensuring their loyalty to the new Church in the future. Mary Tudor was to find Parliament willing to accept the return of the pope, but not the restoration to the monastic order of its lands and wealth. Thus the Church lost control of education and local welfare and with them, much of its influence.

On occasion, arguments about religion were absorbed into other disputes. The Hanseatic League, for so long dominant in North European trade, suffered when the trading rivalries between its member towns were strengthened by rivalries of religion. In sixteenth-century Scotland, those nobles who objected to the French influence over the young Queen Mary were the first to accept Reformist ways. John Knox attacked the whole concept of female rulers through direct references to the Bible.

The areas which remained loyal to the papacy were also able to benefit politically. In Spain and Portugal, where religious uniformity was so much prized, the Inquisition became a tool as much of the state as of the Church. The hold of governments over their colonists abroad was thus stronger than England was to be able to establish in her new colonies in the late sixteenth and seventeenth centuries. If exploration was begun because of Renaissance curiosity, the resultant empires were maintained by religious and government mechanisms. At the same time, the Protestant countries were able to use their dislike of Rome as an excuse to attack and loot these rich lands. Towards the end of the sixteenth century, Francis Drake regarded assaults on the Spanish wealth as an anti-Catholic duty; and the Dutch freedom fighters made use of the issue of religion to strengthen their nationalist aspirations against the dynastic developments which had put their lands into the control of Spain.

It is possible to argue that, for governments in Europe, the Reformation was a more far-reaching development that the Renaissance itself. The poorest people in some parts of Europe were touched by the one as they had not been by the other. Rulers and governments were compelled by events to take a position on religion, and many of them found political or economic benefits, whether from continued loyalty to the old ways or from commitment to the new. It could also be argued that, after 200 years of debate and discussion about the centrality of mankind in the universe, and about the duty to question and investigate everything, the question of the power and legitimacy of the Christian hierarchy could not escape scrutiny, and thus the Reformation was an inevitable 'next step' for the rulers of Europe.

Questions

1. Is a national Church an essential attribute of a nation state?
2. Consider the view that Luther was only successful because of the confused political and constitutional situation in Germany.

SOURCES

1. DO LUTHER'S TEACHINGS FIT WITH THE RENAISSANCE?

Source A: Dante puts into the mouth of the troubadour Foulquet criticisms of the Church and Rome (around 1314–21).

The city – sprung from him who turned his back
First on his maker, and whose nature, sour
With envy, brings the wailing world to wrack –

Sows and proliferates the cursed flower
Which make the sheep and lambs run wild – for lo!
Their shepherds have turned wolves; and hour by hour

Dust gathers on the Gospels, gathers slow
On the great Doctors, while they thumb and scrawl
O'er the Decretals, as the margins show.

That's the whole lore of pope and cardinal
Alike; to Nazareth that felt the beat
Of Gabriel's wings they give no thought at all.

Yet Vatican and every hallowed seat
That marks in Rome some burial ground where lies
The soldierly that followed Peter's feet

Soon shall be freed from those adulteries.

Source B: Marsilio Ficino discusses God in a Platonic way, 1474.

We are united more closely with God through the joy of love, which transforms us into the beloved God, than through knowledge . . . Furthermore, recognising God, we contract His amplitude to the capacity and concept of our mind; but loving Him, we enlarge the mind to the immense amplitude of divine goodness. There, so to speak, we lower God to our level; here we lift ourselves to God. For we know as far as we comprehend; but we love both what we see clearly and what we expect as the remainder of the divine goodness beyond our clear sight.

Source C: Luther's 95 Theses, 1517.

The revenues of all Christendom are being sucked into this insatiable basilica. The Germans laugh at calling this the common treasure of Christendom. Before long, all the churches, palaces, walls and bridges of Rome will be built with our money. First of all, we should rear living temples, not local churches, and only last of all St Peter's which is not necessary for us. We Germans cannot attend St Peter's . . . Why doesn't the pope build the basilica of St Peter out of his own money? He is richer than Croesus.

Source D: Luther writes to Spalatin, 1520.

It is hard to dissent from all the pontiffs and princes, but there is no other way to escape hell and the wrath of God. If you had not urged, I would leave everything to God, and do no more than I have done. I have put a reply to the Bull in Latin, of which I am sending you a copy. The German version is in the press.

Questions

1. Explain the meaning of the term 'Bull' (Source D) (2)
2. Study Source C. Explain briefly the reasons why the pope needed increased revenues for St Peter's. (3)
3. How different from Source B was Luther's view of God and of mankind's relationships with God? (5)
4. Compare Source A with your own knowledge of the complaints the Reformers made against the Church of Rome. Which of Dante's complaints were to be taken up by the Reformers? (6)
*5. Using these sources and your own knowledge, discuss the extent to which the Renaissance provided the necessary preconditions for the Reformation. (9)

Worked answer

*5. [It is important, in these mini-essays, to make full use of every source as well as showing your own knowledge. There is no harm in going through the sources in the order in which they are printed, or you can group them together if it seems more logical, and comment on each in the light of other information.]

Dante, in Source A, is one of many early Renaissance figures who criticised the worldliness and corruption of the Church; the specific accusation here, that Church scholars are more interested in commenting on the commentaries, rather than studying the Bible, was very much in tune with what Luther and Calvin were to argue later. Source C is also a criticism of the behaviour of the Church hierarchy, but emphasises that the enthusiastic patronage of the arts, which the Vatican so much enjoyed, had repercussions in the fiscal area. The complaint that the Church was collecting too much money was one which would attract widespread support throughout Western Europe. The influence of neo-Platonism, as in the example of Source B, almost certainly had the effect of weakening the Church and thus making the Reformation more probable. The Church was not against Platonic ideas, but the effect of this kind of teaching was to reduce the day-to-day hold which the Church had on its members: people in this kind of personal and intimate relationship with God did not need the trappings of Catholicism, did not buy indulgences, visit collections of relics or even see the need for confession and penance.

Source D, which demonstrates Luther's use of the vernacular and of the printing press, makes a direct link with two key developments of the Renaissance. Those who studied the Bible for themselves were likely to find different, and personal interpretations, with a resulting weakening of the authority of the priests.

Some of the preconditions of the Reformation, however, were not directly linked to the Renaissance. The growing urbanisation of the fourteenth and fifteenth centuries has been identified as one of the developments which weakened the status of the Church; the horror of the Black Death may have similarly caused a weakening in Catholic conviction. Nevertheless, without the Renaissance, the Reformation might have been merely another unsuccessful heresy.

SOURCES

2. RELIGION AND THE POLITICAL PHILOSOPHY OF THE RENAISSANCE

Source E: Giovanni Pico della Mirandola writes in 1486 about the centrality of man.

God . . . therefore took man . . . and, assigning him a place in the middle of this world, addressed him thus . . . The nature of all other beings is limited and constrained within the bounds of laws prescribed by me. You, constrained by no limits, in accordance with your own free will, in whose hand I have placed you, shall ordain for yourself the limits of your nature. I have set you at the worlds centre so you may more easily observe the world from there . . . I have made you neither of heaven nor of earth, neither mortal nor immortal so that . . . you may fashion yourself in whatever shape you prefer. You shall have the power to degenerate into the lower forms of life, which are brutish. You shall have the power, out of your soul's judgement, to be reborn into the higher forms, which are divine.

Source F: Deathbed speech of Pope Nicholas V, 1455.

Only the learned, who have studied the origin and development of the authority of the Roman Church, can really understand its greatness. Thus, to create solid and stable convictions in the minds of the uncultured masses, there must be something which appeals to the eye; a popular faith sustained only on doctrines will never be anything but feeble and vacillating. But if the authority of the Holy See were visibly displayed in majestic buildings, imperishable memorials and witnesses, seemingly planted by the hand of God Himself, belief would grow and strengthen from one generation to another, and all the world would accept and revere it.

Source G: Francesco Giucciardini (1483–1548) explains what he feels about churchmen.

I do not know a man more disgusted than I am at the ambition, the greed, the unmanliness of the priests . . . yet the position I held under more than one pope has compelled me for my own interest to desire their aggrandisement. But for that, I should have loved Martin Luther as myself, not that I might throw off the laws laid down in the Christian religion as commonly interpreted and understood, but in order to see this gang of scoundrels brought within due bounds – that is, either rid of their vices or stripped of their authority.

Source H: Erasmus in a letter to his friend Wolfgang Capito, 1517.

It is not part of my nature . . . to be excessively fond of life; whether it is that I have, to my own mind, lived long enough, having entered my fifty-first year, or that I see nothing in this life so splendid or delightful that it should be desired by one who is convinced by the Christian faith that a happier life awaits those who in this world earnestly attach themselves to piety. But at this present moment I could almost wish to be young again, for no other reason but this, that I anticipate the approach of a golden age; so clearly do we see the minds of princes, as if changed by inspiration, devoting all their energies to the pursuit of peace.

Questions

*1. Explain in your own words what Pope Nicholas V (Source F) regards as the key to popular belief. (3)
2. Read Source G. What reasons does Giucciardini give for sympathising with the ideas of Martin Luther and yet not being prepared to take action in support of him? (4)
3. Were the ideas expressed in Source E widely accepted by any group in the Renaissance period? (4)
4. How accurate was Erasmus in his 1517 prediction of a golden age of peace (Source H)? (6)
5. Using your own knowledge and these sources, discuss the view that the central issue of both the Renaissance and the Reformation was the place of man upon the earth. (8)

Worked answer

*1. [This question is worth 3 marks, so make sure you explain clearly, making more than one point.]

Since the ordinary people cannot be impressed by the wealth of learning of the Church, according to the Pope, its greatness needs to be shown in other ways. Fine and imperishable buildings will provide a metaphor for the majesty and eternity of the Church and will convince the people. His view that 'a faith sustained only on doctrines' could not endure was one which the reformers were to attack with great success.

5

THE LINKS BETWEEN THE RENAISSANCE AND OVERSEAS EXPLORATION

BACKGROUND NARRATIVE

The process by which European countries explored and claimed lands in other continents began during the period of the Renaissance and the two movements have been associated by many historians (for example, J.R. Hale (1)). There are obvious links to be made between the spirit of curiosity and questioning which animated the thinkers of the Renaissance and the journeys of travellers to distant parts of the world. Exploration was stimulated by the discovery and interpretation of classical texts about the world. The new scientific ideas of the Renaissance informed and were affected by these explorations, and the doubts already expressed about the teachings of the Church were strengthened when the world patently was not as those teachings had always claimed. At the same time, however, the Catholic Church used the new lands as an opportunity to rejuvenate their message. One of the important developments of the Catholic Reformation, the formation of the Society of Jesus, was the result of St Ignatius Loyola's determination to convert all the nations of the world. New economic and political developments, and the status of rulers, were also affected by the amount of territory they held or claimed, whether far away or not, as can be seen in the extraordinary rise of Portugal. While these links are clear, at the same time, the voyages of exploration were the product of much older processes, and arose from motives which do not share the supposed values of the Renaissance.

Throughout the fifteenth century the Portuguese royal family, the House of Avis, sent exploratory expeditions south along the coast of Africa. These voyages were as much a crusade as a scientific study. Beginning in 1418, following the victory over the Moors at Ceuta in 1415, the aim was to reduce the power of the Muslim rulers, by establishing the extent of their dominions to make possible an attack from the rear, and by cutting off the trade, particularly in West African gold which was one of their strengths. Progress was slow at first. The forbidding Cape Bojador (26° N) was not rounded until 1433, and by 1460 (when Prince Henry 'the Navigator', inspiration for these voyages, died) the Portuguese had still only reached Sierra Leone. They did not cross the equator until 1479 or round the southern point of Africa until 1487. The arrival of da Gama in India (1498) was the culmination of a process which had lasted almost a hundred years. Subsequent voyages reached the Spice Islands of the Moluccas, and as far as Japan and China by the middle years of the sixteenth century.

By the time the Portuguese arrived in India, they were not the only power involved in overseas exploration. The Castilians, too, had a crusading victory as the inspiration of their first involvement. When, in 1492, the centuries-long Reconquista of the Muslim lands of Spain ended in victory at Granada, Isabella expressed her gratitude to God by sponsoring Columbus to carry out the voyage he had been talking about for ten years. His four voyages between 1492 and 1504 claimed the islands and mainland of Central America for Castile, and provided the bridgehead from which the Spanish took over the empires of Mexico and Peru and were able to rule almost all of Latin America until the nineteenth century. Columbus was not the only Italian employed in exploration by the monarchs of Europe. In the 1490s, Vespucci, a Florentine, travelled both for Spain and for Portugal and John Cabot persuaded Henry VII to sponsor an expedition across the North Atlantic. Twenty years later, Francis I of France authorised a voyage by Giovanni da Verrazzano, which began the interest in North America which France was able to maintain until the late eighteenth century, and which survives in the language and culture of parts of Canada. The extent to which this Italian presence is related to the Renaissance in Italy is a matter of debate.

Most of the technical developments which made possible these longer voyages were the result of practical seamanship, rather than theory. (2) The kind of astrolabe needed for navigation, for example, was a very different instrument from those used for the study of astronomy.

Nevertheless, Renaissance developments influenced and were affected by the voyages of exploration. Books about the newly discovered lands were printed in large numbers and avidly read. The reputation of Amerigo Vespucci was, according to Frederick Pohl, (3) tarnished merely because a speculative printer looking for a good story took his account of his two voyages, as written in letters to his Medici patrons, and expanded it to four voyages, one of which was supposed to predate Columbus's landing on the mainland of America. Thus what was printed became the accepted version of events which had, in fact, been very different.

Exploration also formed part of the process of national development which marked the Renaissance period. The status and wealth promised by foreign empires helped to develop national awareness, and provided a theatre in which national rivalries were played out. Francis I famously rejected the papal Bull of 1494 which divided the world between Spain and Portugal, demanding to see 'the clause in Adam's Will' which disinherited France from the rest of the world. The interest of rulers was crucial: in England, the death of Henry VII was followed by a forty-year break in voyages of exploration, which were only resumed when Edward VI came to the throne and the Muscovy Company was formed to try to find the elusive North East Passage to Asia.

It may reasonably be suggested, therefore, that no study of the Renaissance is complete without a consideration of the simultaneous world exploration. The two analyses which follow are concerned with two aspects of these parallel developments.

ANALYSIS (1): CAN THE MOTIVES OF COLUMBUS AND OTHER EXPLORERS BE DESCRIBED AS 'MODERN' RATHER THAN 'MEDIEVAL'?

When Columbus applied to Isabella for the funds to make his long-planned voyage, he hoped to prove that Ptolemy was right, and that the

Atlantic, separating Europe from Asia, was both narrow and navigable. Evidence from the Middle Ages certainly supported this view. Albertus Magnus (?1200–80) had argued that, since there were elephants both in Asia and in Africa, the Atlantic must be no wider than the distance an elephant could swim. Columbus had corresponded with mathematicians such as Toscanelli about the circumference of the earth, and the probable eastward extent of Asia, and these calculations appeared to support his thesis. But, of course, all such theories were firmly rooted in the axiom that the Book of Genesis was an accurate description of the world, and that therefore there was only one land mass. (4) Thus Columbus's supposed scholarship was that of the medieval universities and not of the Renaissance. Columbus's appeal to Isabella was a religious one: he pointed out that his name, Christopher, Christ carrier, made it appropriate that he should take the word of God to the heathen. It seems likely that in her crusading euphoria, the Queen of Castile was impressed by this argument. Historians of the twentieth century have been less impressed. Hans Koenig (5) depicts Columbus as a relentless slaver and racist as far as it is possible to be in attitude from a Christian missionary; and while Felipe Fernandez-Armesto (6) is less hostile, he identifies Columbus's main motivation as being for earthly wealth and status. Columbus's claims were enormous and, had he actually found Asia, impossible to meet: to be admiral of the Ocean Sea is one thing; to be hereditary governor of all the lands discovered, and to take a substantial percentage of the revenue in perpetuity is quite another. A later Spanish adventurer was to summarise his own motives in words which might well be Columbus's: when asked why he had come to the New World, the conquistador Bernal Diaz replied, 'to serve God and the King, and to become rich as all men desire to do'. (7) Nineteenth-century historians argued that the Renaissance encouraged men to see themselves as individuals, and to better themselves by the use of their own abilities rather than relying on God alone. Perhaps we may say that Columbus was inspired in this way: on the other hand, the desire for personal wealth is not one which is limited to any particular period. It has also been suggested that a desire for personal fame and status can be more closely linked to the tales and heroes of the age of chivalry, such as Mallory's *Morte d'Arthur*, enjoying a new popularity as printing made the stories more accessible. In Spain the equivalent legends are those of the Reconquista, and in particular the exploits of Amadis. The conquistadores' amazement on first seeing the wonderful capital of the Aztecs, Tenochtitlan, was expressed by Bernal Diaz: 'It is like the enchantments they tell in the legends of Amadis. Are not the things we see a dream?' (8)

If the motivations of most of the Spanish explorers and conquerors appear to be far from those of the Renaissance, there are exceptions. Amerigo Vespucci had been brought up at the heart of the Renaissance, in Florence; as a younger son, he had avoided the traditional curriculum of the university, being educated instead for commerce and diplomacy. He worked for one of the branches of the Medici family, and his patron was willing to release him when he wanted to see for himself these lands which Columbus claimed were parts of Cipangu and Cathay. He had studied the earlier travel books, and would be able to compare Columbus's lands with the descriptions of Marco Polo, William of Rubruck and others. Reading Vespucci's meticulously detailed accounts of the native peoples he encountered, it is clear that he was consumed with curiosity. So too was the Piacenzan Pigafetta who sailed with Magellan in 1519, and whose account of the first circumnavigation of the globe is full of excitement and close observation. Of course they were interested in profit; but for prosperous and established Italian citizens there were surer ways of making money than long-distance exploration.

The European voyages of exploration had begun with Portugal, for the purpose of defeating the infidel. It is not clear at what stage, if at all, the religious and military motives were superseded by scientific ones, although a contemporary of Prince Henry the Navigator, Diogo Gomes, wrote: 'When Prince Henry wanted to obtain information about the more distant parts of the western ocean, in order to find out whether islands or a continent were to be found outside the world described by Ptolemy, he despatched caravels at a certain time to discover land.' (9) If Henry and the Portuguese were curious, they were also aware of the commercial advantages of reducing the Muslim hold on African, and ultimately Asian, trade. Henry did not hesitate to use the proceeds accruing from the voyages, for example, from the slave trade, to finance further expeditions, and by the time the Portuguese monarchs had handed over exploration to the merchant Fernão Gomes, the main motive was clearly profit. Da Gama, on reaching India, announced he had come to seek 'Christians and spices'.

As late as the last years of the sixteenth century, religion and profit can be seen working together; we may assume that a strong motive for the English explorers like Drake was the need to oppose Catholic Spain in any world arena since, as he circumnavigated the world, he spent time plundering the Spanish settlements along the Pacific coasts of America, and claiming lands (New Albion, for example) for England.

Finally, we should consider whether these explorers made use of the new learning in a practical way. Certainly, as has been said, descriptions of the voyages were widely read, and studied along-side the great works of the Middle Ages. Some of the Renaissance scholarship may even have had the effect of retarding the exploration. Ptolemy's view of the world, popularised by the Renaissance, suggested impenetrable areas north and south of the temperate zone, too cold and too hot to sustain life. It is possible that this slowed down the Portuguese advance southwards. Paradoxically, when the theory was proved wrong in the south, it was also held to be wrong in the north, and many years were wasted, notably by the British, looking for passages north-east and north-west of the land masses of Europe and America. The suggestion that there must be such passages, to harmonise with those of the south-east and south-west, is a particularly Platonic concept. But as for the actual mechanisms of exploration, these owed more to the traditions of European seamanship than to scientific research and development. Columbus never mastered the use of the astrolabe, and became convinced that the mouth of the Orinoco River, which he designated the earthly paradise, lay at the top of a protuberance in the earth's surface, like the top of a pear, or a woman's nipple. His ignorance, and his instinctive methods of navigation contain little of the Renaissance. At most, it can be said that the Portuguese willingness to accept influences from the Arab and Northern European methods of sailing ships shows an open-mindedness which might be said to be of Renaissance style. But in general, as at any time when governments have to be cajoled into sponsorship, the search for knowledge did not feature as strongly as the search for spiritual, political or economic gain.

Questions

1. How far is it possible to identify the motivations of the explorers from their actions?
2. To what extent did the technical developments of the Renaissance affect exploration?

ANALYSIS (2): HOW DID EUROPE'S VIEW OF THE WORLD CHANGE DURING THE FIFTEENTH AND SIXTEENTH CENTURIES?

Educated Europeans in the early fifteenth century certainly knew about some of the other parts of the world. The wealthy of Europe purchased and enjoyed goods from Africa and Asia, and read with interest travel stories, whether fictional, like those of the supposed English knight Sir John Mandeville, or factual, such as Marco Polo's. During the period of Renaissance exploration, however, their world more than doubled in size, and radically changed its form. Columbus found land exactly where he expected to: but the land he found was not Cipangu (Japan) but the flanking islands of an apparently unsuspected continent. The Vikings had visited this land; Bristol merchants are thought to have sighted it. (10) Yet, until 1492, no-one seriously considered the possibility that there was more than one land mass in the world. By the end of the sixteenth century, this was fully accepted, though not finally proved, and the shape of the continent was still a matter for speculation. The Bailly Globe of 1530 shows the 'sea of Verrazzano', to the west of the sandbanks south of Chesapeake Bay. As Morison says, 'thus Verrazzano assumed that he had sighted the Pacific Ocean across an isthmus much narrower than that of Panama'. This tremendous error continued to appear on maps for a century or more. (11) On the other side of the world, it was not till the voyage of Magellan that the Ptolemaic theory of the enclosed Indian Ocean was fully disproved.

The value of these foreign finds were rapidly recognised, though only one nation made serious and enduring attempts at colonisation. As Lomax suggests, only Spain, with its long years of Reconquista, had the techniques required for the government of an alien population:

Within fifty years [Spain] conquered most areas from Texas to Argentina, and established the framework of political, religious, social and economic life within which they would henceforth live. No other European society could have done this at that date. Explorers from England, for example, discovered Nova Scotia in 1497, but no permanent English settlement was made in America until the seventeenth century. Only Spain was able to conquer, administer, Christianise and Europeanise the populous areas of the New World, precisely because during the previous seven centuries her society had been constructed for the purpose of conquering, administering, Christianising and Europeanising [the Muslim south]. (12)

Thus, Lomax suggests, Spain's success was rooted in medieval rather than in Renaissance institutions. The debates aroused by the empire were recognisably humanist, however. Vitoria's lectures at the University of Salamanca, given in the presence of King Charles V in the 1530s, explored issues of natural justice and the right of conquest, even if humanist theory made little impact on the brutal facts of life in Latin America. The international envy which was aroused was also an expression of Renaissance national status, as other powers, notably the English and later the Dutch, expressed their enmity for Spain in attacks on her overseas territories.

The effects on the economies of Renaissance Europe were enormous and far reaching. The first country to feel these effects was Portugal, even before it became clear that they were aiming for India: 'in the 1450s the profit on a Mauritanian slave was estimated at 700 per cent'. (13) The ways in which rulers used such profits were as might be expected in Renaissance Europe: to enhance the power of the monarchy in the face of the nobles. 'The wealth of Africa was garnered by John II who ascended the throne in 1481. He used it to build up the power of the monarchy against the nobility.' (14) The commercial shape of Europe changed, as the focus moved from the Mediterranean to those nations which faced and could use the Atlantic Ocean, although the Mediterranean never completely lost its trading status, despite all that Portugal could do to close the Red Sea and Persian Gulf routes. Portugal's empire lifted her into the ranks of the major powers of Europe. In Spain, the effects were even greater. As J.H. Elliot demonstrated, (15) the wealth of America caused the flowering of a golden age before ultimately destroying the Spanish economy. The Habsburg monarchs were able to commission extra-ordinary works of art and architecture; but at the same time the huge amounts of bullion arriving in Spain, and the distorting effect on agricultural, industrial and social institutions, worsened and prolonged the galloping inflation. Like King Midas, the Spanish governments found themselves with unlimited gold which was still insufficient to sustain their policies.

For the other powers of Europe, the new discoveries were, through-out the Renaissance period, a focus of envy more than anything else. France and Britain resented and tried to encroach upon the holdings and the trade of the Iberian powers, the French even making settlements in Portuguese Brazil during the 1560s, while the British desperately searched for routes to Asia not yet monopolised by Spain. Support from Elizabeth I for the Portuguese independence struggle against Spain was not disinterested.

As mentioned earlier in this chapter, the voyages of exploration provided material for the hungry printing presses of Europe, and at the same time provided inspiration for the writers and poets of the late Renaissance. Epic poetry and adventure stories took exploration as their theme; Shakespeare clearly used material from accounts of the voyages as inspiration. For example, Caliban's god, Setebos, in *The Tempest* (16) shares a name with one of the gods of the Patagonians of southern Argentina, and his unlovely appearance echoes Pigafetta's descriptions.

The ordinary people of Europe may not have had the education to recognise the changing geography of the world, or the leisure to enjoy the stories of wild and wonderful places and people, but their lives were being changed just the same. The population increase would not have been sustainable without the new staple crops coming from America. It is hard to imagine Northern Europe without the potato, or Southern Europe without maize and its products. Similarly, the increased availability of sugar and cotton soon affected life at every level in society.

Of the many changes which affected Europe in the fifteenth and sixteenth centuries, those brought about by the voyages of exploration were among the most significant. And yet it took many years for these changes to be absorbed into the lives of Europeans and the policies of their governments. Not till the eighteenth century did non-European issues dictate policy within Europe, rather than the other way round; nor did the ordinary people of Europe appear at once to be aware that they were living in a suddenly larger and more diverse world than a few decades before.

Questions

1. How true is it that, for the ordinary people of Europe, the voyages of exploration had little impact?
2. Consider the view that the economic effects of the voyages of exploration radically altered the balance of power in Europe.

SOURCES

1. RENAISSANCE INFLUENCES ON THE EXPLORERS AND THEIR SPONSORS

Source A: Cadamosto describes why he went exploring, 1455.

[Prince Henry] had caused seas to be navigated which had never before been sailed and had discovered the lands of many strange races, where marvels abounded. Those who had been in these parts had wrought great gain among these new peoples, turning one soldo into six or ten. They related so much in this strain that I with the others marvelled greatly. They thus aroused in me a growing desire to go thither.

Source B: Luis Vaz de Camoens imagines the classical gods taking an interest in da Gama's voyage, 1572.

Up on Olympus, the Gods were assembling in Council to consider future happenings in the East. Jupiter had sent his summons out by Mercury, and now from North, South East and West, down the Milky Way they came, treading the crystal skies, leaving to their own devices all the seven spheres entrusted to them by the Supreme Power, who governs heaven, earth and angry sea by thought alone.

Source C: Ferdinand Columbus describes his father's clever use of scientific knowledge in Jamaica, 1502.

At the rising of the moon the eclipse began, and the higher it rose, the more complete the eclipse became, at which the Indians grew so frightened that with great howling and lamentation they came running from all directions to the ships, laden with provisions ... When the Admiral‾ perceived that the crescent phase of the moon would soon shine forth clearly, he issued from his cabin, saying that he had appealed to his God for them and had promised Him in their name that henceforth they would be good. God had pardoned them, in token of which they would soon see the moon's anger and inflammation pass away.

Questions

1. Explain the reference to the 'seven spheres' in Source B. (3)
2. What 'marvels' had in fact been found by the time Cadamosto (Source A) was writing? (4)
3. How convincing do you find Camoens' (Source B) evocation of a classical backdrop for the voyage of da Gama? (4)
*4. Comment on the tone and content of Ferdinand's account of his father's trick (Source C). (7)
5. What do these sources tell you about the interplay between classical education, medieval legend and the explorations of the Renaissance period? (7)

Worked answer

*4. [It is important to be sure to answer both parts of the question, so that the points you want to make accumulate all the marks there are.]

Ferdinand Columbus's account of his father's life is always adulatory, and Columbus is always, as here, referred to as 'the Admiral'. The event is made to sound very exciting, with dramatic language being used to describe the hysterical reaction of the native people, in contrast to the magisterial calm of the Admiral himself. Ferdinand clearly implies that this piece of cunning solved all Columbus's problems, and ensured that provisions and assistance were forthcoming from then on.

It is surprising to read of Columbus successfully using science to help him out of his difficulties. These events occurred when he was trapped by his own incompetence on Jamaica. At this stage he was still claiming that Cuba was part of the mainland of Asia, despite having sailed all the way round it. His understanding of the lands he had found was always limited, and had more to do with his dreams than with actual observation and deduction.

His contemptuous treatment of the natives here is typical of his reaction to them: however much he claimed to be there on behalf of God, he himself enslaved and abused the native people, and never attempted to impose good behaviour on his subordinates. The strong implication that he was in control of the situation runs counter to all other accounts of his experiences during his fourth voyage.

SOURCES

2. SOME EUROPEAN VIEWS OF THE WIDER WORLD

Source D: Sir John Mandeville, *circa* 1360.

And you must understand that in this land, and in many others thereabouts, the star called Polus Arcticus cannot be seen; it stands ever in the north and never moves, and by it seamen are guided. It is not seen in the south. But there is another star, which is exactly opposite the first star; and seamen steer by that star there as here they do by the Pole Star. Just as their star cannot be seen here, so our star cannot be seen there. It can be seen from this that the world is quite round; for the parts of the firmament which can be seen in one country cannot be seen in another. It can be proved thus. If a man had adequate shipping and good company, and had moreover his health and wanted to go and see the world, he could traverse the whole world above and below . . . and return to his own country . . . That could well be, even if men of limited understanding do not believe that men can travel on the underside of the globe without falling off into the firmament. For just as it seems to us that those men there are under us, so it seems to them that we are under them. For if it were possible for a man to fall off the earth to the firmament, all the more reason for the earth and the sea, which are very heavy, to fall thither too.

Source E: Letter from Robert Thorne, written from Spain, 1527.

Of the new trade in spicery of the Emperor, there is no doubt but that the islands are fertile of cloves, nutmegs, mace and cinnamon, and that the said islands with other thereabout abound with gold, rubies, diamonds, jacynths and other stones and pearls as all other lands that are near or under the equinoctial.

Now then, if from the said Newfoundlands the sea be navigable, there is no doubt but, sailing Northwards and passing the Pole descending to the equinoctial line, we shall hit these islands and it shall be a much shorter way than either the Spaniards or the Portuguese have . . .

But it is a general opinion of all cosmographers that . . . the sea is all ice and the cold so great that none can suffer it. And hitherto they had all the same opinion that under the equinoctial line for much heat the land was uninhabitable. Yet since by experience is proved no land so much habitable nor more temperate, and to conclude, I think the same should be found under the North if it were experimented. So I judge there is no land unhabitable nor sea innavigable.

Source F: Richard Hackluyt describes the reasoning behind the Muscovy Voyage of 1553.

At what time our merchants perceived the commodities and wares of England to be in small request with the countries and people about us and near to us, and that those merchandises were now neglected and the price thereof abated, certain grave citizens of London began to think with themselves how this mischief might be remedied. Seeing that the wealth of the Spaniards and Portuguese, by the discovery and search of new trades and countries was marvellously increased, supposing the same to be a course and mean for them also to obtain the like, they therefore resolved upon a new and strange navigation. After much speech and conference together it was at last concluded that three ships should be prepared and furnished out, for the search and discovery of the northern part of the world, to open a way and passage to our men for travel to new and unknown kingdoms.

Source G: Acosta tries to explain species diversity, 1590.

It is . . . difficult to determine the origin of the various animals that are found in the Indies and are not found in the Old World. Because if the Creator brought them forth there, there was no need to have recourse to Noah's Ark, nor would it even have been necessary to save all the species of birds and animals then, if they were to be created anew afterwards . . . it must also be considered whether such animals differ specifically and essentially from all the others, or whether their difference is accidental, which could be caused by various accidents, as among the family of man some are white and others black, some are giants and some dwarfs. Thus, for example . . . in the sheep family . . . some are large and strong with very long necks like those of Peru, others small and weak and with short necks as those of Castile.

Questions

1. What are the modern terms for 'Polus Arcticus' (Source D) and 'equinoctial' (Source E)? (2)
2. To what extent does the content of Source D suggest that it was written before rather than during the Renaissance? (4)
3. How does modern science explain the problems posed in Sources D (why men do not 'fall off' the earth) and G (the diversity of species)? (5)
4. How far do these sources suggest that there was real curiosity in Europe about the newly discovered lands? (6)
*5. Using these sources and your own knowledge, discuss how complete a summary of the prerequisites for voyages of exploration can be found in Sources D, E and F. (8)

Worked answer

*5. [The words 'how complete' should alert you to the fact that you are required to find all the prerequisites mentioned in the sources, and then go on to consider any not mentioned here: hence the generous allocation of marks for this question.]

The writer Sir John Mandeville (Source D) lists several prerequisites for voyages of exploration: he suggests that good shipping and competent manpower are essential, together with good health and a will to find new things. When the voyages began, health soon proved to be a problem as the unprecedented length of the voyages led to deficiency diseases, in particular scurvy. As far as good men are concerned, Columbus had problems with his officers and his crews on each of his voyages, and yet achieved some success. Aside from these problems, his list is not complete, since he ignores the need for backing money and trade goods.

Source E accepts by implication the need for a solid motive before expeditions will be paid for, and suggests that the potential profits of such a journey would be enough to produce the essentials of money and commodities to be risked for trade.

Both Thorne and Hackluyt (Sources E and F) suggest the nationalist dimension of these voyages, since both regard competition with the

Iberian powers as an issue. If strong motivation is a prerequisite, then these sources are incomplete, since they do not refer to the religious impetus which drove the Portuguese around the coast of Africa and sent Columbus across the Atlantic.

Implied in all these sources is the extent to which academic reading and research backed up the planning of voyages; these writers have a sound knowledge of geography as it was studied during their times.

6

SCIENTIFIC CHANGE IN THE RENAISSANCE

BACKGROUND NARRATIVE

The desire to understand how the world worked was inherent in the learning of the Renaissance, and therefore it is not surprising that important scientific developments occurred during the fifteenth and sixteenth centuries. The methods which are now seen as being scientific were the methods which were applied to all aspects of life: questioning the existing order of things and using observation to test accepted authority. At the same time, the new technologies of the Renaissance, themselves in part the result of scientific research, made change more likely and assisted in the spread and cross-fertilisation of ideas. The need for technological support helps to explain why, in the main, the scientific developments followed those in the fields of art, architecture and literature, and stretched over longer periods than is expected in modern science.

Mathematics was not subject to technological constraints, and was encouraged by the translation of Euclid in the twelfth century, with the concept of proof being rapidly accepted, and the most important development came from the Renaissance interaction between the Arabic and Christian worlds. The adoption of the Arabic numeral system, with the concept of zero, was initiated by merchants, in the thirteenth century, who appreciated the added flexibility and ease of computation. During the sixteenth century Gerolamo Cardano (1501–76) found the solution to cubic and quartic equations, and algebraic analysis was extended by François Viete (1540–1603).

Changes in the general field of biology can be seen to be linked to the artistic Renaissance, since accurate anatomy was a prerequisite for the realism of the great painters. Dissection and detailed study overturned many of the inaccuracies which had been accepted because they were associated with Aristotle and other authorities of classical times. When Andreas Vesalius (1514–64) published *The Structure of the Human Body*, he was able to incorporate a large amount of new knowledge upon which others could base their research. In 1578 Fabricius described the valves in the heart, but continued to accept Galen's view that blood ebbed and flowed to and from the heart in both veins and arteries. As Christopher Marlowe had written in 1590:

Your artiers which alongst the veins convey
The lively spirits which the heart engenders (1)

Only in 1628 was William Harvey able to take the next step, and describe the circulation of the blood and the differing functions of veins and arteries. The way these biologists worked was, when allowance is made for the equipment they had, precisely the way that modern scientists work. No microscope was available until the mid-seventeenth century, when Leeuwenhoek (1632–1723) was able to reveal, among other things, the fibres in eye lenses, and the structure of the epidermis. While new discoveries about the human body were being made, however, few changes occurred in the actual practice of medicine, and the Galenic teaching of the four humours continued to dominate, except where translations of Arabic texts extended the understanding of the more educated physicians.

Agricultural, as opposed to human, biology has always been subject to gradual change, and the most significant developments in this area were not to occur until the late seventeenth century. The introduction of new crops from the New World during the sixteenth century, notably the new staples of North and South Europe, the potato and maize, may perhaps have facilitated the acceptance of fodder crops such as turnips which were to revolutionise stock production in the future.

Cosmology was based on the Alexandrian of the second century AD, Ptolemy, as confirmed when his great *Cosmographia* had been translated in the twelfth century. The earth was at the centre of the universe, with the planets and stars orbiting around it, held in eight crystal spheres which controlled their movements. Ptolemy reported that the planets appeared to move backwards at times, and explained this by suggesting that they orbited some fixed point (in an epicycle) as well as passing round the earth. This view was rejected by Copernicus (1473–1543) in his *De Revolutionibus Orbium Coelestium*, which was published in 1543. From Copernicus onwards, the Greek tradition ceased to dominate astronomy. He argued that the earth, with the other planets, moves round the sun, although the orbits he attributed to them were unduly complex. Both Tycho Brahe (1546–1601) and Johannes Kepler (1571–1630) elaborated on and, indeed, questioned his work. Not until Galileo obtained a novelty item from the Netherlands could the heliocentric system be fully demonstrated. This arrangement of mirrors and magnifying glass, which became known as a telescope, enabled Galileo to watch the moons of Jupiter orbiting the planet, and thus clearly not fixed upon the crystal sphere. The explanation of why the planets were held in their relationship to one another had to wait till the late seventeenth century, and Isaac Newton's exposition of gravity. It is interesting to note that the gradual acceptance of new ideas in astronomy did not change the work or status of astrologers: clearly, whatever moved in the heavens, whether it was the sun or the earth, the zodiacal influences were still regarded as significant.

Developments in optics and in glass making had also meant that from the later years of the fifteenth century magnifying spectacles for short sight were comparatively common at just the same time as books became more readily available and cheaper. Technological advances also made possible further discoveries in science, for example, when Torricelli (1608–47) demonstrated existence of air pressure and when von Guericke (1602–86) used an air pump and his 'Magdeburg hemispheres' to create a vacuum.

Of all the sciences, only chemistry made no perceptible advance during the centuries of the Renaissance. All the key ideas of the ancient world were still held by the end of the sixteenth century: the recognition that substances change their nature, but that there are some substances which are irreducible; the idea that there were four elements, earth, air, fire and water; these classical ideas were accepted throughout the Renaissance. Such books as were written, for example, by Biringuccio (1540) and Agricola (1556), were practical treatises on mining, based as much on Pliny as they were on observation, and summarised all existing knowledge. The paints and dyes used by artists and craftsmen were those known in classical times. No new substance, unknown to the Greeks, was isolated until 1670 with the identification of phosphorus, and it was only in the eighteenth century that nitrogen, hydrogen, oxygen, nickel, cobalt and many others were found and named. The reasons for this lack of change during the Renaissance were in part technical: accurate measurement, both of time and of substances, was essential and this was not possible before the eighteenth century. A more important reason may, however, be the attitudes of the chemists themselves. Having demonstrated that substances change in amazing ways: that a red rock can produce a strong grey metal, or that by mixing two metals (reddish copper and grey tin) a golden-coloured metal (brass) is produced, alchemists were convinced that anything was possible, in particular the transmutation of base metals into gold. This dead-end research wasted centuries and, perhaps more significantly, set chemists against governments, who were afraid of the destabilising economic effects of possible success and cheap gold. (Pope John XXII had banned the study of alchemy in 1317.) When scientists also searched for a substance which would have a similar effect on human life itself, they entered the province of the Church, and the hunt for the elixir of eternal life labelled them as dabblers in magic and therefore dangerous.

Thus the foundations for the modern scientific methods of precise observation and detailed recording were laid, with the major exception of chemistry, during the Renaissance, and the technical developments begun then ensured that discoveries would continue and be disseminated. The growth of world trade, the increase in town populations, the weakening of the intellectual hold of the Church, all these changes aided and were aided by new methods of looking at the world and by the perceptions of how the world worked. The two analyses which follow consider the relationship between the Church and scientific change, and the extent to which Renaissance science was modern in its theories and methodology.

ANALYSIS (1): WAS THE CATHOLIC CHURCH RIGHT TO TREAT DEVELOPMENTS IN SCIENCE AS A THREAT?

The Catholic Church faced many threats to its authority during the Renaissance period. Its authority had for may years stemmed from its control of access to eternal life, and also its domination of education and the means of social advancement. Aspects of the Renaissance threatened this status in many ways: 'The return of intellectual debate to the community, the spread of printing, and the concomitant expansion of the educated class all contributed to the development of a lay intelligentsia much larger than that of the medieval universities and Church.' (2) This lay intelligentsia listened to the Reformers, and read the works of Luther and Calvin. The educated class studied with interest the travellers' tales of Vespucci, Columbus and others, and noted the differences between the geography described by these explorers and what they had been taught. They debated bases for government other than that of divine appointment. It is in this context of general questioning of authority that we need to consider the extent to which the position of the Church was actually threatened by scientific developments.

The scientists, like the artists and explorers, sought to explain the world around them in rational and logical terms. Indeed, the division between the artists and the scientists was not clear cut. Leonardo da Vinci pondered aspects of theology and nature in what may be seen as a truly scientific way, considering whether the biblical account of the Flood was possible with reference to the properties of water. All the artists analysed nature. In their attempts to depict exactly what they saw, they made use of rules of mathematics and practised close observation. Experiments with pigments and with new methods of bronze casting are two of the reasons why some of Leonardo's works have not survived. He, like other artists, applied scientific methods to his art. 'Art, then, could not cheat nature but, by discovering, obeying and manipulating natural laws, with increasing quantification and measurement, art was seen to deprive nature of her mysteries.' (3) The Church, in its dealings with ordinary people, had traditionally preferred to rely on a sense of mystery, and of the inexplicable nature of the workings of the Almighty. While in the universities and among the great thinkers of the medieval Church, a harmony had been achieved through all fields of thought between Christian and classical traditions, this was not extended to parish level. Any explanations of the detailed mechanisms of the natural world could be seen to weaken the popular view of divine omnipotence. Eventually, during the seventeenth century,

Descartes and Newton were to describe a creator who developed and left running a magnificent machine; but in the fifteenth and sixteenth centuries, God was perceived as having a more intimate involvement with the day-to-day workings of the world.

Chemists were already marginalised by the association of their work with magic, or with economically risky tampering with the value of gold. The study of medicine did not change sufficiently to be perceived as a threat. Issues of the definition of life and death were not to engage the attention of theologians as well as doctors until the latter part of the twentieth century. The Church, as it had in the Middle Ages, attempted to prevent the practice of dissection, but increasingly licensed this kind of study, particularly when it was the artists they themselves employed who needed to do the research. The papacy made use of the new achievements of perspective and realism when it commissioned Michelangelo to paint the Sistine Chapel ceiling.

The new geographical discoveries were also accepted. The papacy took up the challenge posed by the existence of previously unknown peoples by authorising missionary work to convert them. There was little point in claiming that they could not exist, since they are not listed in the survivors of Noah's Ark, when it was clear that they did exist. So the scientific questions posed by the enormous variety of human and animal life in the New World were not directly addressed, except by individuals such as the Jesuit José de Acosta (?1560–1600). (4)

If new discoveries in biology and geography were not seen as a threat by the Church, the new developments in astronomy certainly were. The geocentric universe was a prerequisite for the whole of the Church's message about the 'loving purposes of God in Christ'. (5) Having created the whole universe, God had chosen the earth as the focus of His attention, and had therefore regularly to forgive and excuse the appalling behaviour of his creatures. The concept that the earth was merely one of many planets, moving as they did, was clearly blasphemous. The early heliocentric astronomers, like Copernicus, were working in theory alone. Like the Greeks, Copernicus looked for something that was logical and simple: his explanation required fewer different orbits than Ptolemy's and was therefore, he thought, more likely to be true. Theory was the province of universities and thinkers and did not pose a serious threat to the Church. But Galileo, from his observations in 1609–10, claimed to have visual, physical evidence that the heavens were not as the Bible claimed. The Church utterly rejected these ideas, and used all its earthly power to silence Galileo: he was forced to retract and then was imprisoned indefinitely, remaining under house arrest until his death in 1642. The Church only accepted the validity of his work formally in 1993. It rapidly, however, became the accepted view among the educated and among other scientists. In the Protestant countries his views were used as proof of the reactionary and illogical attitudes of the Roman Church, though even in Protestant countries it took time to give up the traditional geocentric model. At the beginning of the eighteenth century, Joseph Addison (1672–1719) described how the planets and stars 'in solemn silence all Move round the dark terrestrial ball'. (6) For the ordinary people, whether heavenly bodies move in heliocentric or geocentric orbits was scarcely of daily importance. The evidence of their own eyes appeared to support the one as well as the other. But as these ideas came to be discussed and accepted, there was an accompanying weakening in respect for the Church which continued to deny them.

By the mid-sixteenth century, the Papal Index offered loyal Catholics a list of books which were dangerous to their souls. Comparatively few of the books listed in the first century of its existence were, however, scientific works. Similarly, the Holy Office of the Inquisition, although it dealt with Galileo, was far more concerned with theological dissidents than with scientific ideas. Indeed, the Society of Jesus, recognising the significance of the new scientific ideas, was among the first educational institution to include a study of astronomy and physics in its curriculum.

Rightly or wrongly, religion has continued to feel threatened by scientists, as it had during the Renaissance. In the last two centuries, the attack has come particularly from the biologists, rather than the astronomers. Darwin's account of evolution, now virtually universally accepted as reliable, appeared to relegate the early books of the Bible to the status of fiction and therefore to attack the existence of God. Richard Dawkins in the 1980s (7) made this attack more overt and, in the last years of the twentieth century, new methods of creating life, such as cloning, also appear to call into question the premises on which religion is based. Modern faiths, just like the Church in the Renaissance, have had to look for ways of accepting and dealing with new ideas and approaches, particularly since, in the end, a valid scientific idea can be proved, leaving any institution which rejects it appearing slightly ridiculous and certainly anti-intellectual. It is not true to say that Renaissance churchmen viewed all scientific ideas as threatening. They accepted, and indeed used, many: and those which they did reject and attempted to suppress survived regardless of their antagonism.

Questions

1. To what extent did the new ideas in science influence the ordinary people of Europe in the fifteenth and sixteenth centuries?
2. Consider the view that the threat posed by scientific theories was the least of the worries of the Church in the Renaissance.

ANALYSIS (2): HOW 'MODERN' WAS SCIENCE DURING THE PERIOD OF THE RENAISSANCE?

Definitions of 'modern' science are inevitably problematic, although it is possible to find clear discussions of the various issues. (8) For the purpose of this analysis, we may simply say that modern science suggests models, or hypotheses, and relies on repeated testing of these hypotheses by accurate measurement and experimental precision. Publication, in journals which are read by other scientists, helps to test results and achieve consensus. This rigorous approach is increasingly paralleled by ever-improving worldwide communications, such as the Internet, so that controversies like the solution to Fermat's last theorem, or issues of bioethics can be discussed by the whole scientific community, if not by the whole population. We should also note that much of the income of modern science derives from the interplay between 'pure' research and its commercially viable applications.

Scientists of the Renaissance usually based their work on the writings of the ancients. Many publications took the form of commentary upon classical works, as Copernicus expressed his views in terms of adjustments to Ptolemaic cosmography. They also regarded harmony as a key test of the validity of their theories. The perceived balance between the different elements and their properties, wet and dry, hot and cold, healthy and sick, were assumed to be the basis of life. As Joan Solomon says, 'when a scientific theory gets well established in a society over a long time, everyone comes to rely upon it and its predictions, even if they do not understand it'. (9) Questioning the existing theories and looking for new patterns which explained illogicalities were the mechanisms by which new theories were formed, then as now. Galileo's doubts about the work of Brahe and Kepler pushed him towards his own conclusions, assisted by his precise observations.

Measurement and experimental precision were not easy for the scientists of the Renaissance. The inability to measure small units of time precisely affected experimental results, although books such as *The New Attractive* by Robert Norman, published in 1581, described detailed and thorough experimental work. Norman had conducted a wide range of experiments to explain magnetism. Advances in chemistry had to wait till the eighteenth century before glassware and measurement devices were of an adequate accuracy, although scientists were aware of and tried to overcome this problem. Jan van Helmont (1577–1644), for example, used careful measurements of water, and accurate weighing in his attempt to discover the origin of the living tissue of trees. Where technical advances were made, they were used, as Galileo used the telescope.

Communications improved radically during the Renaissance years. Travel around the coasts of Europe became safer as maps improved, and the medieval tradition of students travelling to study abroad was enhanced by the growth of a substantial educated urban class.

John Dee complained that in the 1540s, finding no appropriate expertise in England, he had had to learn his mathematics on the continent . . . It was partly due to his enthusiastic promotion that by the end of the century English mathematical science was thriving, with many books published in the vernacular and a new instrument making centre established in London. (10)

Above all, printing made the dissemination of information much cheaper and easier. Specialist texts in many fields of science were published, such as Gilles de Corbeil's *De Urinis*, which was published in 1484. Renaissance doctors shared the conviction of the classical writers that urine was a useful diagnostic tool, and de Corbeil's book offered them much useful advice. More general and infinitely more influential, was the publication of Andreas Vesalius's *De Humani Corporis Fabrica* in 1543, which provided a detailed and accurate account of the human body and replaced many of the myths put forward by the ancient Greeks. It was still the case that technical and scientific books were published in Latin, thus giving them an inter-national readership. While these mechanisms do not compare with the electronic communication and dissemination methods of modern times, they were worlds away from the mechanisms of the Middle Ages.

The commercial derivations of scientific work were limited in the Renaissance period.

Mathematicians came to see their subject as characterised by progress, one whose techniques could be beneficially applied in a number of related practical disciplines known as the mathematical sciences. On the strength of their successes in navigation, cartography and surveying, they asserted its importance and widespread relevance. (11)

Some applications of astronomy were also used in navigation and cartography; but these were more in the nature of gadgetry than original theories. Medical men did not make much use of the gradual discovery of the details of human anatomy, not least because it continued to be true that 'medicine was in many respects a domestic art'. (12) A medical textbook printed in 1484 quoted the homely advice of previous generations: 'The best physicians are Dr Diet, Dr Quiet and Dr Merryman.' (13) But it was also because surgeons did not have the high status accorded to physicians, and physicians continued to rely on the work of the ancients.

The attitudes of Renaissance scientists were in many ways those of modern science. They asked questions, and postulated answers which they attempted to demonstrate by experiment or by observation and examples. They retained, however, the classical and medieval view that harmony and simplicity alone were the best tests of any new theory or development, where modern science would have additional criteria. Their methods could not be modern, since levels of accuracy and speed of recording and dissemination were beyond their technical reach. And the financial benefits of science were more dependent on the generosity of patrons than on the applicability of what they discovered or deduced.

Questions

1. What do you consider to be the most important achievements of Renaissance science?
2. To what extent was the development of Renaissance science limited by technological inadequacies?

SOURCES

1. CHANGING VIEWS OF THE UNIVERSE

Source A: Nicholas of Cusa (1401–64).

I have long considered that this earth cannot be fixed but moves as do the other stars . . . to my mind the earth revolves upon its axis once in a day and a night.

Source B: Cardinal Nicolaus von Schoenberg to Nicolas Copernicus, 1536.

You not only profoundly understood the teachings of the ancient astronomers, but . . . also constructed a new world system. You teach, as I have heard, that the earth is moving and that the sun occupies the centre of the world, and that the eighth heaven, the firmament, remains constant and motionless, and that the moon together with the elements of its sphere between Mars and Venus revolves about the sun in an annual orbit.

Source C: Girolamo Cardano (d.1576).

Nothing comes closer to human happiness than knowing and understanding those things which nature has enclosed within her secrets. Nothing is more noble and excellent than understanding and pondering God's supreme works. Of all doctrines, astrology, which embraces both of these – the apotheosis of God's creation in the shape of the machinery of the heavens and the mysterious knowledge of future events – has been unanimously accorded first place by the wise.

Source D: Sir Henry Wotton to the Earl of Salisbury, 1610.

The Mathematical Professor at Padua [Galileo] who by the help of an optical instrument (which both enlargeth and approximateth the object) invented first in Flanders and bettered by himself, hath discovered four new planets rolling about the sphere of Jupiter, besides many unknown fixed stars; likewise the true cause of the Milky Way, so long searched, and lastly that the moon is not spherical but endowed with many prominences and, which is of all the strangest, illuminated with the solar light by reflection from the body of the earth as he seemeth to say. So as upon the whole subject he hath first overthrown all former astronomy . . . and next all astrology.

Questions

*1. Explain in your own words Galileo's conclusions about the moon, as described by Sir Henry Wotton in Source D. (2)
2. What did the 'ancient astronomers' (Source B) teach about the heavens, and how did Copernicus change these views? (4)
3. On what grounds could fifteenth-century observers such as Nicholas of Cusa (Source A) conclude that the stars move and that the earth revolves? (5)
4. Compare the views expressed about astrology in Sources C and D. In the light of other information you have about the period, which do you think is the more accurate view? (6)

5. Using these sources and your own knowledge, discuss the view that changes in cosmography were only of relevance to the intellectual classes of Europe. (8)

Worked answer

*1. [The purpose of this question is merely to ensure that you have understood the language used by Wotton. This means that you should focus on the more difficult words.]

According to Source D, Galileo has concluded that the moon has hills and valleys upon it, rather than being a smooth globe; also, that rather than having its own light, as suggested in the Book of Genesis, it is lit by the light of the sun.

SOURCES

2. CHANGING VIEWS OF NATURE

Source E: A painter's apprenticeship contract, 1467.

And he must teach him how to foreshorten a man's head by isometry, that is of a perfect square underneath in foreshortening, and to teach the method for making a nude body, measured both from the back and from the front, and to place eyes, nose and mouth in the head of a man in their correctly measured place . . . and to give him always a paper of examples in hand, one after the other of different figures, to highlight and to correct the same examples and to correct his mistakes.

Source F: Leonardo da Vinci on the subject of Noah's Flood.

Here a doubt arises, and that is as to whether the flood which came in the time of Noah was universal or not, and this would seem not to have been the case for reasons which will now be given. We have it in the Bible that the said flood was caused by forty days and forty nights of continuous and universal rain, and that this rain rose ten cubits above the highest mountain in the world. But consequently, if it had been the case that the rain was universal, it would have formed in itself a covering around our globe which is spherical in shape; and a sphere has every part of its circumference equidistant from its centre and therefore . . . it becomes impossible for the water on its surface to move, since water does not move of its own accord unless to descend. How then did the waters of so great a flood depart if it is proved that they have no power of motion? If it departed, how did it move unless it went upwards? At this point natural causes fail us and therefore, in order to resolve such a doubt, we must needs either call in a miracle to our aid, or else say that all this water was evaporated by the heat of the sun.

Source G: Leonardo da Vinci discusses flight.

A bird is an instrument working according to mathematical law, which instrument it is within the capacity of man to reproduce with all its movements, but not with a corresponding degree of strength, though it is deficient only in the power of maintaining equilibrium. We may therefore say that such an instrument constructed by man is lacking in nothing except the life of the bird, and this life must needs be supplied from that of man.

Source H: Andreas Vesalius describes the decline of medicine, 1543.

After the devastation of the Goths particularly, when all the sciences, which had previously been so flourishing and had been properly practised, went to the dogs, the more elegant doctors at first in Italy in imitation of the ancient Romans began to be ashamed of working with their hands, and began to prescribe to their servants what operations they should perform upon the sick, and they merely stood alongside after the fashion of architects . . . and so in the course of time, the technique of curing was so wretchedly torn apart that the doctors, prostituting themselves under the names of physicians, appropriated to themselves simply the prescription of drugs and diets for unusual affectations; but the rest of medicine they relegated to those whom they call chirurgians and deem as if they were servants.

Questions

1. Explain in your own words the division in the practice of medicine described by Vesalius (Source H). (2)
*2. What does Source E tell us about the relationship between art and the study of mathematics and science? (4)
3. What can be learned from Source F about the extent of Renaissance understanding about the properties of water? (4)
4. To what extent, in Sources F and G, does Leonardo da Vinci question the accepted teachings of the Church? (6)
5. Using these sources and your own knowledge, discuss the extent to which science in the Renaissance was able to explain the workings of the world. (9)

Worked answer

*2 [It is sensible to make several points when there are four marks at stake, so you need to look beyond the issue of measurement and find some other topics to mention.]

Source E clearly recognises the importance of accurate measurement, which was also being recognised as crucial in the sciences of the period. The proper placing of the features was recognised to be a matter of measurement. The use of the correct formula to achieve accuracy in perspective is also referred to, as is the need for observation and accurate recording. In addition, the utility of examples and of repeated practice is made clear, and the general tone is that art is teachable and correctable, like any science. The division between art and the practice of science was one which occurred much later.

7

THE NORTHERN RENAISSANCE

BACKGROUND NARRATIVE

At very much the same time as the Renaissance was developing in Italy, major changes were occurring in other parts of Europe. We have already seen that ideas in science were being discussed in Northern Europe; and the impetus for the voyages of exploration came from Portugal and Castile, rather than from any of the Italian states, even if the explorers themselves were Italians. The term 'Northern Renaissance' is most frequently used with reference to the Netherlands, but it is relevant to consider Western Europe as a whole.

The fifteenth-century dukes of Burgundy, whose lands included the Low Countries, were among the richest rulers in Europe. Their lands straddled the trade routes linking the Mediterranean with the North, and thus they were able to dominate the exchange of crucial commodities, naval stores and fish from the North, and the textiles and foodstuffs of the South and East. The wealth of the duchy was celebrated in a flowering of art which many would regard as comparable with developments in Italy. The sculptor Claus Sluter was renowned for his realistic figures, and painters such as Jan van Eyck (?1389–1441) achieved the effect of distance without the mathematical 'linear perspective' methods of the Italians by using precise details and a range of rich tones of colour. The art of Flanders was discussed and imitated all over Europe. Other noted artists of the Netherlands and Flanders include Rogier van der Weyden

(?1400–64) and Hieronymus Bosch (?1450–1516), whose symbolic paintings have an almost surreal appearance. By the end of the fifteenth century, political and dynastic links were being made with the Habsburgs, which were to result in the absorption of Burgundy into the wider empire first of Maximilian and then of Charles V. These links, together with marriages involving the royal families of Portugal and Spain, ensured that the Netherlands had links with every corner of Europe.

In many of the German states trade wealth could be spent on embellishing both religious life and the town halls of the free cities. Printing became the chief mechanism of religious debate and of the Reformation. The Northern universities led the way in the new astronomy, with Copernicus from Poland, and Kepler from Germany.

France experienced a flourish of building and artistic ideas. Well before the involvement in Italy began in 1494, architecture and art had enjoyed royal patronage. Later, Francis I was able to entice the ageing Leonardo da Vinci to retire to the royal town of Amboise. At the same time, however, the pursuit of a grandiose foreign policy was to prove expensive, and the religious divisions of the Reformation culminated in a civil war which affected France for much of the latter part of the sixteenth century.

In Castile and Aragon, Renaissance developments occurred alongside religious fervour of the kind more usually associated with the Middle Ages. Ferdinand and Isabella both expelled the Jews and strengthened the Holy Office of the Inquisition; at the same time, however, they encouraged the foundation of new universities, such as that at Alcala, and sponsored the publication of the so-called Polyglot, or parallel-text Bible, as an aid to scholarship. The motivation for the sponsorship of Columbus may have been that of crusaders; but the effects were revolutionary. The art of El Greco (1541–1614) shows the same balance between religion and innovation: the subject matter of his paintings was usually religious, but the Inquisition was worried by the distorted and elongated bodies of the holy subjects he portrayed, and he was subject to the scrutiny of the Holy Office. It is perhaps for this reason that the great flowering of Spanish art was delayed until the seventeenth and eighteenth centuries and beyond. Meanwhile, in Portugal, in the two centuries during which the House of Avis resisted the aggression of Castile, the study of mathematics and astronomy was applied to the business of trade and exploration, and scholars were welcomed regardless of their religion or ethnicity. In many ways, Prince Henry 'the Navigator' was a medieval figure, living as he did the life of a monk; but his curiosity and willingness to learn from any source is distinctly Renaissance.

The whole of Europe outside Italy saw significant developments in every intellectual field during the period of the Renaissance. The first of the two analyses which follow considers the issue of whether the non-Italian and Italian Renaissances were distinctive, or part of a united whole; the second focuses on the distinctive characteristics of the English Renaissance.

ANALYSIS (1): IS IT TRUE THAT THE ARTISTIC RENAISSANCE IN THE NORTH WAS IMITATIVE RATHER THAN ORIGINAL?

People involved in the artistic Renaissance elsewhere in Europe were aware of, and impressed by, ideas in Italy. Many of them expressed a willingness and desire to travel. Erasmus's 'longing for Italy' was a feature of his letters to his friends, and at the same time there was a widespread recognition of the benefits of learning from the experiences of others. This has meant that 'Northern' and Italian art, their aims and ideals, are almost invariably elided, making them seem to pursue similar if very general goals – such as an interest in individual consciousness, and a desire to make images of the visible world, often portraying a religious scene, more believable and accessible.' (1)

There were many contacts between the artists of the North and those of Italy, as well as with those of other parts of Europe. Noble and commercial travellers to Italy ensured that Italian works of art were brought north, and were admired and displayed. Artists and works of art travelled in both directions. After all, artists travelled to where there was work to be done and, more particularly, their works went to where there was a purchaser for them. Jan van Eyck, for instance, travelled to Portugal and Spain several times, initially because he had been commissioned to paint the bride-to-be of the Duke of Burgundy. Meanwhile, Rogier van der Weyden painted a portrait of Francesco d'Este of Ferrara during the time when he was attached to the Burgundian court. In 1483, the Medici Bank's representative in Bruges, Tommaso Portinari, presented to the church of Sant' Egidio (in the ospedale of Santa Maria Nuova in Florence, founded by his family in the thirteenth century) an altar piece by Hugo van der Goes. At the same time, there are many common features. Personal portraits, whether of the patrons or of the artist and his acquaintances, were often included, both in Italy and in the North. An early example is Adam Kraft's depiction of himself as one of the figures holding up his pulpit in Nuremberg (c.1493–6); similarly, Michelangelo was to put various of his friends, and enemies, into his interpretation of the Last Judgement for the Sistine Chapel. The inclusion of the people who had paid for the picture is one source for historians for portraits of otherwise unrecognisable people. For instance, the Vespucci family are depicted in a painting by Ghirlandaio of the Holy Family (1472), which provides the only known portrait of the man for whom America is named.

It is, however, an oversimplification to suggest that the European artistic Renaissance was all one movement, as there are many differences. Patrons in the North, apart from the rulers, tended to be bourgeois, rather than religious or noble, and the pictures which they commissioned were therefore often for civic or even domestic display, as well as for churches or palaces. Guilds commissioned works for their halls and chapels. Perhaps for this reason, the works are often on a smaller scale than those produced in Italy: the triptychs of van der Weyden and van der Goes are much smaller than many Italian wall and altar paintings. A further instance of the more economic scale of Northern works is the frequent use of grisaille, to simulate a sculptural effect, on triptych covers.

Frescoing was less common than painting on wooden panels in the North, and speculative painting or carving was quite common, in contrast with the emphasis on commissioned works in Italy. This may be explained, perhaps, by a combination of the commercial and physical climates in Flanders. The artists, like the merchants, were skilled in finding markets, and were adept at producing items which would create as well as meet public demand. Small and portable works of art could be shown where they might be purchased, in the same way as other commodities. At the same time, fresco takes longer to dry in the damper and colder climate of the North and, in the darker North, windows are larger and therefore of more interest to artists.

The subject matter, too, is distinctive. 'Northern artists and patrons seem acutely and even minutely aware of their current or potential social position. Some Italian artists do exhibit a degree of social consciousness, but it does not seem to be of such overriding importance in Italy as in the North.' (2) One of the comments often made about the Northern Renaissance is that realism is the central focus. On the other hand, examples abound which demonstrate that symbolism is central. The greatest symbolic artist of the period, the German Hieronymus Bosch, worked mainly in the North, although he visited Italy in 1505. His *Garden of Earthly Delights* (1505–10), hung in the palace of the Regent of the Netherlands and, like his *Ship of Fools*, bears little resemblance to any of the works of the Italian Renaissance.

Among the more 'mainstream' painters, however, symbolism was also an essential element. Holbein's *The Ambassadors* is crammed with significant objects which help to display the status of the subjects and their intellectual interests. In van Eyck's famous *The Arnolfini Wedding* realism has been sacrificed to the symbolic nature of the picture. The chandelier, as is often pointed out, is hung so low that anyone entering the room would bump into it. But the point is to display the wealth of the groom, rather than to depict his room. Similarly, the expensive mirror is not at an angle at which it could actually be used. The inclusion of personal and domestic details, both in the background and in the actual subject matter of the picture, is also characteristic of Northern art. Italian artists were less likely to include small objects of everyday use in their depictions of great classical or biblical scenes, or in their portraits of their noble and wealthy patrons.

The Reformation, as it took hold in the North, had the effect of moving the emphasis from the depiction of the saints and traditional stories of the Catholic Church to more secular and down-to-earth subject matter. The robust work of the Brueghel family (Pieter Brueghel, ?1520–69) demonstrates this as much as does the change to more formal paintings of the seventeenth century.

The art of the Northern Renaissance contained many unique features. The artists were eager to learn from Italy, but their techniques, subject matter and pattern of patronage ensured that the pictures they produced were never mere imitations of the works of the great artists of the South.

Questions

1. What were the distinctive features of the Renaissance in the North?
2. How true is it to suggest that commerce, far more than diplomacy, controlled links between the different artistic movements in Europe?

Plate 5 *The Ambassadors: Jean de Dinteville and Georges de Selve*
(1553) Hans Holbein the Younger. Photo © National Gallery, London

ANALYSIS (2): WHAT WERE THE KEY FEATURES OF THE ENGLISH RENAISSANCE?

In many ways, Renaissance developments in England were different from those elsewhere. No single artist achieved renown in England throughout the period of the Renaissance, although towards the end of the sixteenth century artists of note, such as Nicholas Hilliard, produced works which may be termed mannerist, building on the basic traits of the Renaissance. This is not to say that there was no interest in art in the British Isles. Admiration for Italy was widespread; the purchase of paintings in Italy and the commissioning of Italian artists were ways in which the prosperous classes chose to spend their money. Similarly, artists from abroad were invited to work in England. Although the English monarch was not able to imitate the feat of Francis I in persuading Leonardo da Vinci to settle in France, Hans Holbein did some of his best work at the court of Henry VIII.

The growing nationalism recognised as an element in the Renaissance was less striking in England, because of its distinctive history. David Starkey writes,

> as a territory, England was already old; it had an unbroken political history since at least the Norman Conquest of 1066, and the limit of legal memory stretched back to the beginning of the reign of Richard I in 1189. It was also an unusually centralised and well-governed Kingdom, with the result that it was probably more aware of itself as a unity than any other area of comparable extent in Europe. (3)

Thus, while the monarchs of Europe were striving to build themselves national states, and to expand their territories, England, once it had finished with the Wars of the Roses, was enjoying stability in foreign policy and never seriously attempted to recover the lands in France lost in the fourteenth and fifteenth centuries. It is true that the last holding in France, the pale of Calais, was not lost until the middle of the sixteenth century, but the effect was less than might have been expected, since trade was increasingly focused towards the Netherlands and towards the new markets in the west. Mary I may have claimed to have 'Calais' written on her heart, but the loss of the territory was a result of her involvement with the policies of the Habsburgs rather than those of England. Henry VIII was willing to share in the kind of international ostentation which accompanied the negotiations at the 'Cloth of Gold', but his international stature never approached that of the rulers of France or Spain. The 'standing army' of England, the Yeomen of the

Guard, was never more than a royal bodyguard, and the defence of England continued to rely on the part-time training of citizens in the militia. This contrasts with the huge expenditure on mercenaries or on standing armies of other Renaissance rulers.

The pattern of patronage was different in England, as well. During the fifteenth century, the interest of the Lancastrian rulers encouraged humanist studies, and book collecting: for example, the library which was to form a part of the library of Oxford University. The sixteenth century saw a development unique to England, when the wealth and land of the monasteries was channelled into the building of country homes embellished with the ornaments of the Renaissance. Monarchs had built palaces, notably Henry VII's Richmond and Henry VIII's Hampton Court, but all over England the new and the old nobility competed in the building of houses ranging from the modest improvements at Hever Castle to the glories of Longleat House and Hardwick Hall. New cathedrals and town halls were the achievements in Italy and in Flanders; in England fine domestic buildings occupied the architects and interior designers, many of them invited from Italy.

Issues of religion preoccupied the thinkers of England, in a way which was fraught with danger elsewhere in Europe. Thomas More chose death rather than renounce the Supremacy of the pope; but this did not stop him from criticising the abuses of the Church in several writings of which the most notable is *Utopia*. John Colet, in establishing (1509–12) his school at St Paul's, declared that he did not mind whether the teachers were clergy or not, as long as they could teach the best Latin and Greek. A clear and accurate translation of the Bible was commissioned by Henry VIII, and it was his choice as Archbishop of Canterbury, Thomas Cranmer, who did much of the work of translating the Catholic mass into English. Where Germany and France were torn by religious wars, and Spain and Italy were held in the Catholic Church by the benefits of church patronage and the work of the Holy Office of the Inquisition, the Church of England, by the decision of Henry VIII, changed its allegiance with only localised and short-lived resistance.

The English Renaissance is often deemed to be a literary one. Geoffrey Chaucer's writings have been said to mark the beginning of vernacular literature in Northern Europe; but it was the theatre which marked England's Renaissance as unique. In other countries theatres were built in palaces and chateaux, for the entertainment of the aristocracy and the kings. In England theatre was a popular medium. Travelling players were welcomed with as much interest as the guild religious plays. The plays they performed were written for a mass audience: the stories were lurid and full of exciting characters. Dramatic events occurred on stage, rather than being reported as they were in the classical plays so much admired in the Renaissance period. The scenery was sketched in the words, since there was not the money for lavish design or effects. Although the first permanent theatres were not built until the 1570s, play-going had been established for several decades. The poems of the period were created for a more select market; the patrons of the poetry of Spenser and Shakespeare were the courtiers of Elizabeth I and the subject matter that of love and chivalry. The courtiers themselves, such as Walter Raleigh and Philip Sydney, were proud to be recognised as poets rather than merely sponsors of the work of others.

Exploration, as far as England was concerned, was more a matter of trade and profit than of a search for knowledge. During the fifteenth century, the Bristol merchants had sailed far into the Atlantic in search of cod (or stockfish as it was known once it was salted and dried to form a staple part of the winter diet of Europe). Henry VII encouraged John Cabot, and later his son Sebastian, to explore, but there was then a pause, during the reign of Henry VIII. It has been suggested that the Muscovy Company of the 1550s was motivated by curiosity, since they continued their investment long after the North East Passage to Asia had been found to be impassable and costly in lives and equipment. At the same time, the influence of John Dee, and his interest in navigational methods, may confirm a link between mathematical theory and the business of seeking new markets and commodities.

It is reasonable to suggest that England enjoyed, to some extent, all the elements which the Renaissance displayed in other parts of Europe. During the fifteenth century, preoccupations with civil war delayed the adoption of Renaissance change in England, but by the end of the century the exchange of ideas was accelerating. If there were no home-grown painters and sculptors, nevertheless, the visual arts flourished through importation, and an interest in architecture has left Britain with a significant body of fine buildings. At the same time, writing of all kinds, from religious tracts and political satire to popular plays and beautiful poetry, marked the high point of Northern Renaissance literature. Technical developments like printing, and the new methods for exploration, were rapidly adopted in England. While the patrons were not necessarily noble, nevertheless, they were prepared to spend their wealth on intellectual and artistic projects. Thus, even if it was later and slighter than in Italy, we may say that England enjoyed its own distinct Renaissance.

Questions

1. How much of the distinctiveness of the English Renaissance do you consider is the result of England's geographical position?
2. 'Monarchs had less influence on the taste of their wealthier subjects in England than elsewhere in Europe.' How far do you consider this statement to be true?

SOURCES

1. LINKS BETWEEN ITALY AND THE NORTHERN RENAISSANCE

Source A: Vasari describes Northern influences on the work of Andrea del Sarto (1486–1530).

None the less, his figures, despite their simplicity and purity, were well conceived and without errors, and in all respects utterly perfect. The expressions of the faces he painted, whether boys or women, are natural and graceful, and those of his men, both young and old, are done with vivacity and splendid animation while his draperies are a beauty to behold, and his nudes are very well conceived. And although he drew with simplicity, his colours are none the less rare, and truly inspired . . . I shall not leave out that while Andrea was engaged on these and other pictures, there were published some copper engravings by Albrecht Dürer and Andrea made use of them, taking some of their figures and reproducing them in his own style.

Source B: A contemporary of Lucas Cranach comments on his work.

You paint people who seem alive and whom everyone recognises immediately at sight . . . you painted the virtuous Duke John so admirably that, not once but repeatedly, the people of Lochau, upon entering the castle and seeing through the window just the upper half of the picture, bared their heads and knelt to him as is their custom.

Source C: Michelangelo's views on Flemish art (recorded by Francisco de Hollanda).

Flemish painting . . . will, generally speaking, please the devout better than any painting of Italy, which will never cause him to shed a tear, whereas that of Flanders will cause him to shed many . . . It will appeal to women, especially to the very old and the very young, and also to monks and nuns and to certain

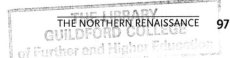

noblemen who have no sense of true harmony ... They paint stuffs and masonry, the green grass of the fields, the shadow of the trees, and rivers and bridges, which they call landscapes, with many figures in this side and many figures on that. And all this, though it pleases some persons, is done without reason or art, without symmetry or proportion, without skill, selection or boldness, and finally without substance or vigour.

Source D: The German Albrecht Dürer visits Antwerp and Brussels, September 1520.

The church of Our Lady at Antwerp is so very large that many masses are sung in it at one time without interfering with each other. The altars have wealthy endowments, and the best musicians are employed that can be had. The church has many devout services, much stonework and in particular a fine tower. I have also been into the rich abbey of St Michael. There are, in the choir there, splendid stalls of sculptured stonework. But at Antwerp they spare no cost on such things for there is money enough ... at Brussels is a very splendid town hall, large, and covered with beautiful carved stonework ... I saw the things which have been brought to the king from the new land of gold, a sun all of gold, a whole fathom broad, and a moon all of silver of the same size.

Questions

1. Explain the reference (Source D) to 'the new land of gold'. What political and dynastic developments had ensured that these things were on display in Brussels? (4)
*2. Does Source A provide adequate evidence to show that Italian artists were keen to learn from the Northern artists? (5)
3. Comment on the validity of the criticisms supposedly levelled by Michelangelo at Flemish art (Source C). (7)
4. Using these sources and your own knowledge, discuss the differences between sources of patronage in the North and in Italy (9)

Worked answer

*2. [The short answer to this question is clearly 'no': but to earn the marks, you need to discuss all the clues you are given here.]

The craft of copper etching was developed to a high standard in the German printing towns like Munich, and was used to make copies of works of art. It is to these that Vasari is referring, when he describes Andrea del Sarto being able to take and use Dürer's figures in his own work. But at the same time, etchings of Italian works were circulating in the North, ensuring that such influence flowed both ways. Vasari clearly feels that del Sarto was impressed by Dürer's work, but this kind of copying was acceptable in the Renaissance workshops of the artists. Vasari does not make clear whether del Sarto was the only artist who was impressed by, and who used, the work of Northern artists. One example is clearly not enough to distinguish a trend. Much of Vasari's writing, like this, is anecdotal rather than closely researched and totally reliable.

SOURCES

2. ASPECTS OF THE RENAISSANCE IN ENGLAND

Source E: Erasmus writes to John Colet about scholasticism, 1499.

It is not that I condemn their learned studies, I who have nothing but praise for learning of any sort, but these studies are isolated, and not seasoned with references to any well-written works of an older age . . . they exhaust the intelligence by a kind of sterile and thorny subtlety, in no way quickening it with vital sap or breathing into it the breath of life; and worst of all, by their stammering, foul and squalid style of writing, they render unattractive that great queen of all sciences, theology, enriched and adorned as she has been by the eloquence of antiquity. In this way they choke up, as it were within brambles, the way of a science that early thinkers had cleared and, attempting to settle all questions, so they claim, merely envelop all in darkness.

Source F: Thomas More (*Utopia*) on farming, 1516.

For one shepherd or herdsman is enough to eat up that ground with cattle, to the occupying whereof about husbandry many hands were requisite. And this is also the cause that victuals be now in many places dearer. Yea, besides this the price of wool is so risen that poor folk, which were wont to work it and make cloth of it be now able to buy none at all. And by this means very many be fain to forsake work and to give themselves to idleness. For after that so much ground was enclosed for pasture, an infinite multitude of sheep died of the rot, such vengeance God took of their inordinate and insatiable covetousness, sending among the sheep that pestiferous murrain, which much more justly should have fallen on the sheep masters' own heads.

Source G: John Dee writes about Number, 1570.

How immaterial and free from all matter Number is, who doth not perceive? . . .
To deal with a science whose subject is so ancient, so pure, so excellent, so
surmounting all creatures, so used of the almighty and incomprehensible wisdom
of the Creator in the distinct creation of all his creatures: in all their distinct
parts, properties, natures and virtues, by order and most absolute Number
brought from nothing to the formality of their being and state. By Number's
property, therefore . . . we may . . . draw ourselves into the inward and deep
search and view of all creatures' distinct virtues, natures, properties and forms
and also farther arise, climb, ascend and mount up (with speculative wings) in
spirit to behold in the Glass of Creation the Form of Forms, the Exemplar
Number of all things numerable, both visible and invisible, mortal and immortal,
corporal and spiritual.

Source H: Shakespeare's Miranda expresses her amazement at the world.

O wonder
How many goodly creatures are there here
How beauteous mankind is! O brave new world
That has such people in't.

Questions

1. Explain in your own words how, according to Thomas More (Source F), God punished the greed of sheep owners. (3)
2. Study Source E. How far did Colet share Erasmus's views on scholasticism, and to what extent may these views be said to be 'typically Renaissance'? (5)
3. How far do you agree that John Dee's glorification of 'Number' demonstrates that the Renaissance was beyond the reach of the ordinary people? (7)
*4. Using your own knowledge, discuss the extent to which these sources encapsulate the key elements of the English Renaissance. (10)

Worked answer

*4. [Each of these sources needs to be considered, and then you should go on to discuss aspects of the Renaissance in England which are not referred to in them.]

Source E reminds us first of all that the link between England and foreign scholarship was a key aspect of the Renaissance, and that men like John Colet ensured that English education would develop and would focus on the beauty of classical Latin and Greek, and the study of humanist topics. The reference to theology also suggests that, in the North more than in Italy, issues of religion and the Church would form a central part of Renaissance debate. Source F concerns the economic and political input of English thinkers. More was not alone in choosing to comment on the developments which were affecting and damaging everyday life. The poet John Skelton had satirised many of the issues which More later dealt with in his writings. John Dee's eminence throughout Europe as a mathematician, astronomer and astrologer prefigured the way in which, in the next century, English students of science and mathematics were to develop and advance the work of earlier astronomers. John Dee may be said to be a forerunner of Newton, Herschel and the great English scientists of the eighteenth century. Shakespeare, putting into the mouth of his heroine a wonder at the beauties of creation, is just one of the great English poets and playwrights of the later sixteenh century.

In England, then, the Renaissance developed later than it had done in Italy and in the rest of mainland Europe; its focuses were literary and scientific to a much greater extent than they were artistic: although European artists were employed by the wealthy in Britain, and although the latter imported art works as they travelled through Southern Europe, native artists of any note did not emerge until the latter part of the sixteenth century, in the style commonly labelled as mannerist, rather than Renaissance. The political and religious emphases of the English Renaissance may well have arisen from developments in England: the creation of the Book of Common Prayer being the best known, bringing together great writing, scrupulous translation and theological debate.

8

DID THE RENAISSANCE CHANGE EUROPE?

BACKGROUND NARRATIVE

The study of the Renaissance was more straightforward in the nineteenth century than it is today. Jacob Burckhardt (1818–97), in his great work *The Civilisation of the Renaissance in Italy*, argued that the Renaissance saw the birth of man as an individual. In his view, every aspect of life was changed by this great movement. In the century since his death, historians in every field have preferred to identify continuities, and thus the history of dramatic revolutionary change has become unfashionable. Nevertheless, the two centuries generally accepted as the Renaissance period (for instance, Roy Porter and Mikuláš Teich define the Renaissance from the mid-fourteenth to the end of the sixteenth century (1)) saw major changes in every sphere of European life. Porter and Teich, indeed, claim, 'the movement obviously constituted a great turning point in the history of the West'. (2) Methods of scholarship changed for ever. New technologies both facilitated the exploration of the heavens and ensured that new discoveries would be widely publicised. New techniques as well as new aesthetic perceptions changed the way buildings for the rich and their protégés were made, whether secular or religious. The economies of most regions of Western Europe were affected by the discovery of new markets, new commodities and new foodstuffs. By the end of the sixteenth century, for example, maize was being used in much of Southern

Europe and the potato had been introduced to the areas of Northern Europe where it would soon become a staple.

Until the fifteenth century, books were costly treasures, each copy requiring months of skilled labour; between 1450 and 1500 20 million books were printed, representing up to 15,000 titles. During the sixteenth century, 200 million books were published. While a strengthening of national identities encouraged the use of native languages, printing may well be a more important factor in ensuring the growth of vernacular languages, and the end of Latin as a vehicle for all but the most formal transactions. On the other hand, we may consider that the humanists themselves brought about the death of Latin: by insisting on the purity of Ciceronian style, they forcibly constrained a language which, throughout the Middle Ages, had been able to develop new vocabulary as the world changed. Once this approach was condemned, and the neologisms rejected, Latin stultified, while the body of literature in many languages, notably German, French and English, as well as Italian, grew and flourished.

By the mid-sixteenth century, in many spheres, innovation had settled into routine. For example, no major geographical discovery was made for over a century after the return of Magellan's voyage (1521), although details of the world were elaborated and explained.

Where Burckhardt had seen the Renaissance as innovation, many historians since have emphasised the continuity of developments. In the 1920s J.W. Allen wrote, 'All through the [sixteenth] century, except at least in Italy, political thought remained essentially medieval in character.' (3) More recently, Christopher Frayling has pointed out that 'in every period there has been an interest in the Middle Ages. In the Renaissance the great poets returned to the themes of knightly sagas' (4) as indeed did the painters and the printers. One of the books published by Caxton was Mallory's *Morte d'Arthur*. Views like these may suggest that the Renaissance was not a discrete period, but merely a series of developments growing out of its own past and continuing into the centuries which followed it. Some writers go so far as to suggest that the Renaissance was merely an expression of the latest fashion of the courts of Europe, and had no impact on ordinary lives at all. At the other extreme is the view that suggests that absolutely everything that happened during the two centuries is linked to the Renaissance. The truth probably lies somewhere between these two views. The two analyses which follow consider whether it is possible to identify a moment that marks the end of the Renaissance, and, secondly, whether this period can be seen in any sense as a turning point in European history.

ANALYSIS (1): WHEN DID THE RENAISSANCE END?

If we say that the Renaissance saw a series of radical developments, in many aspects of intellectual, political, scientific and artistic life, then it is reasonable to suggest that the end of the Renaissance came when innovations had become accepted as the usual method of doing things, and when once revolutionary ideas were regarded as everyday, and were taught in school and university.

In art this 'end' is often seen as coming in the middle of the sixteenth century, when realism and linear perspective had become merely tools of the trade of art. Peter and Linda Murray provided a 'snapshot' of the height of the Renaissance in their evaluation of the most famous image of the Sistine Chapel ceiling:

> Twenty years earlier nobody would have had the technical mastery to create so perfect a human form, like a Greek god; still less would anyone have had so boldly simple a conception of the scene, with the earth no more than indicated behind Adam, and everything concentrated on the expression of Adam's reluctant, sluggish body which is animated by the impulse, like an electric shock, passing down his arm . . . Twenty years later everybody, in imitation of Michelangelo himself, would have given the scene too much energy, too much intensity; the nobility would have disappeared from the conception. (5)

The more mannered and constrained art which developed from the art of the Renaissance is termed 'mannerism' and it rapidly developed, particularly in Northern Europe, and in Spain, into the formal and classical works of the seventeenth century.

One of the reasons for the development of humanism may have been the restlessness and feeling of uncertainty following the Black Death. With the death of one in three of the population of Europe, old certainties were threatened, and new questioning searched for better answers to the difficult problems of human relationships with the world and with God. As the population recovered, which was the case in many parts of Europe by the mid-sixteenth century, so confidence was re-established, and both the Catholic Church and the new Protestant Churches strove to establish their authorities over their followers, in intellectual as in other matters. 'The dominant ideologies of both radical Protestant and traditional Catholic thought privileged the past' (6) and this became the more true as the strife of the Reformation settled into regional stability. By the Confession of Augsburg of 1555 the Reformation was over, or at any rate accomplished, in the sense that the Holy Roman Emperor accepted that the Catholic Church would never regain control in his dominions. The attempts to restore Catholicism in England (by Mary I) or to impose it in Scotland (by the Guise influence) were unsuccessful, as were Spanish efforts to force the Netherlands back into the Roman Church. Education was accepted as important, with rulers founding schools and universities, but it was not made available to the mass of the population unless, as in the Middle Ages, the Church offered basic schooling in the villages. In England, for example, the schools established by Edward VI were almost entirely urban.

In some parts of Europe new nation states had become established during the Renaissance. In Iberia, Castile and Aragon were linked, rather than Castile and Portugal – which for much of the Middle Ages might have seemed the more probable union – and despite Spanish occupation between 1580 and 1640, Portugal was to remain a separate entity. The two significant duchies of Brittany and Burgundy lost their autonomy; although the boundaries of France, to the east at least, were to continue to fluctuate well into the twentieth century, the state of France was established by the peace of 1559 (Cateau Cambresis). By the end of the sixteenth century, the power of the state had increased at the expense of that of the nobles in most of the countries of Western Europe. Indeed, only in a few Northern countries, such as England and Denmark, did the national assemblies retain any significant role in government. If the formation of the nation state is a part of the Renaissance, we may say it was accomplished by the last years of the sixteenth century. The patterns of overseas influence were also set by the second half of the sixteenth century. Renaissance exploration had, by the 1530s, created substantial over-seas 'empires' in the hands of Spain and Portugal. Almost immediately, other European nations had begun to 'trespass' on the lands of the Iberian powers; despite a few modest settlements by the English and French, this was the pattern which was maintained until well into the eighteenth century.

In science, the key step was the rejection of the classical authorities. Although new developments in science occurred later than those in other fields, in 1543 two books were published, those of Copernicus and Vesalius, both of which contradicted the teaching of the ancients in astronomy and biology. Once this step had been taken, other scientific events were inevitable. The key move had been that away from deduction and towards observation and experimentation.

> Aristotle had suggested than the most perfect, universal valid knowl-
> edge . . . was arrived at by deduction, logically correct reasoning
> based on irrefutable axioms. Truth arrived at by simple induction,
> extrapolation from particular instances, was profoundly problematic
> and could be seen as implying nothing more than a high degree of
> probability. (7)

The Church was to condemn Galileo, in part at least because the authorities saw no reason to believe what the telescope appeared to show. But once scientists had begun to think and observe for themselves, new conclusions were bound to follow.

Many of the most significant developments of the fourteenth–sixteenth centuries may be seen as 'economic' rather than 'Renaissance'. Increased urbanisation has been cited as a cause of Renaissance developments; it was certainly to continue unchecked from the sixteenth century onwards. New production methods for metals and for textiles were also adopted during this period; there was no equivalent 'leap forward', until the end of the seventeenth century and the start of the so-called 'agricultural' and 'industrial' revolutions.

Several of the contemporary sources quoted in this book have shown that people living at the time were excited by the changes they were living through. While it is tempting to suggest that this was just the view of the self-publicising élite, David Starkey argues strongly that 'the student of the Renaissance must try to recapture that sense of wonder at another, new world – however devalued, dog-eared or doubtful it seems to have become'. (8) If we do accept that these were exciting times, then we can see that by the later decades of the sixteenth century the sense of excitement had died down, and that systems, ideas and technical developments had been incorporated into everyday life.

Questions

1. What criteria can be used to decide the end date or dates of a set of developments?

2. In the light of your studies of the Renaissance, consider the usefulness to historians of the convention of dividing history up into periods or movements.

ANALYSIS (2): IN WHAT SENSES WAS THE RENAISSANCE 'A TURNING POINT'?

In modern times we should say that any period of 200 years can expect to see major changes in all aspects of life; but this had not been as true of the Middle Ages as it was of the fifteenth and sixteenth centuries. Spheres where developments had been almost imperceptible, or at the least recognisably sequential, now saw changes in completely new directions. Paradoxically, many of these changes began through reference to the distant past. Indeed, 'the ethos of literate humanism was one far more disposed to venerate the authority of the past than to champion innovation'. (9) The Renaissance view of the classical past was a rosy one, since neo-Platonism and neo-Aristotelianism are less élitist than their original, pre-Christian roots, but it had the effect of glorifying town as opposed to rural life, the very word civilisation deriving from the life of towns, and of encouraging patronage of the arts for the greater good of the city state. 'In neo-Aristotelian terms, the Prince or wealthy individual had a duty to spend lavishly on appropriately grandiose works of art.' (10) The growth of towns was seen by Carlo M. Cipolla as the key change which both brought about the Renaissance and allowed it to flourish. Using terms like 'drab' and 'crude' for the life and work of medieval man, he suggested that only in towns could patrons, wealth and artistic innovation come together to create a new world. (11) Developments in art and architecture bear this out. The long, slow development of the Gothic gave way rapidly to classical architecture; realism and linear perspective became the automatic tools of the artist and sculptor; if we exclude Goya, it appears that it was not until the second half of the nineteenth century that artists began seriously to experiment in the area of visual accuracy for the purposes of other 'realisms'. (12)

Scholarship and study changed radically. Focusing at first on the writings of the great authors of Greek and Roman times, Renaissance scholarship soon developed its own intellectual momentum. For the first time since the beginning of Christianity, learning was not confined to institutions controlled by the Church. Topics of study extended to include new views of the world and of government. Education began to be seen as desirable even by the nobles, who during much of the

Middle Ages had been content to leave such matters to their chaplains and chancellors; in many towns schools were established for people of all ranks. Of course, this was possible because of the moderate size of urban populations and their comparative wealth, and it continued to exclude the mass of the rural population; but nobody now claimed that education should be reserved for the élite alone, or only for those destined for the Church. The tools for increased education were available in the vernacular languages which, despite the classical roots of Renaissance learning, now began to dominate; and in the technological achievement of printing. Other developments, such as the pendulum for the study of the earth's rotation, and the compass and portable astrolabe, had more specific influences, but all new learning was publicised and universalised by the printing presses.

As far as knowledge of the earth is concerned, these centuries were certainly a turning point. The Pythagorean and neo-Pythagorean myths of the uninhabitable torrid and frigid zones of the world were dispelled. The question of a single creation was tested by the discovery of so many and so diverse groups of people previously unknown that Vespucci, for one, wondered whether God had repeated his creation on the other side of the Atlantic. The speculations of some thinkers of the later Middle Ages, such as the writer of the fictional *Travels of Sir John Mandeville*, that there is no land unknowable or sea unnavigable, were now demonstrated, with far-reaching effects in Europeans' perceptions of their own place in the world, as well as in agriculture and commerce. The population recovery of the centuries following the Black Death would not have been able to continue without the new foodstuffs brought from America, since agriculture had contracted so radically during the fourteenth and fifteenth centuries that marginal land had returned to the wild.

The changes in Christianity, which are associated both with the new, scrupulous methods of scholarship and with the new interpretations of the Bible and of the Church's teaching made inevitable by new discoveries, also marked a turning point. There had been previous schisms in the Church, but these had arisen from theological disputes among its rulers. Medieval heresies rising from the ordinary members of the Church had been suppressed or marginalised. Now, however, the Church in Western Europe was permanently fragmented because of Luther's close textual study of the Epistles of St Paul in the original language, supported by a population tired of the depredations of the church-building art patrons who were the popes, and spread widely and accurately by the printing press. A comparison with the Lollards, or the Hussites, with their networks of secret travellers carrying precious copies of vernacular scriptures and heretical teachings around Europe, confirms that a change of some magnitude had taken place.

The rulers of Europe were encouraged by humanists to look back with admiration to the rulers of classical times. Popes, kings and emperors wanted the kind of glory and lasting memorials which the Roman Emperors had achieved for themselves. Artists were able to benefit from this quest for aggrandisement: the equestrian statue was an art form which engaged the attention of Michelangelo, Leonardo and others. But at a more serious level, the rulers of Europe also sought territorial and governmental position. Again, the new technologies of war ensured that fighting became a profession, as it had been in Roman times, and specialists in it could command high fees. The establishment of national identities and of 'natural' boundaries was an aim which could be pursued by the new armies. The renewed availability of secular education also moved the day-to-day business of government away from churchmen and into the hands of professionals, including, in some cases, the rulers themselves. The image of Henry VII checking each page of the accounts, or of the Emperor Charles V and Philip II of Spain pursued on their travels by an unending river of paperwork awaiting their attention are typical of the Renaissance.

One field where the ancients were rejected by Renaissance thinkers was that of science. Only by moving away from the acceptance of authority, and the deductive method of argument from universally accepted axioms, could science reach a state in which the developments of later centuries were possible, moving forward and making discoveries by experiment and observation.

Modern empirical science required, as a condition of its possibility, plausible arguments that the ancients knew only imperfectly. Otherwise, while new, independent and direct investigation of nature could have taken place (as of course it had) it would have had to continue to locate itself within the traditional Renaissance ideologies of ancient wisdom. (13)

Despite the fact that scientific change was, in the main, a feature of the century after the Renaissance may reasonably be said to have ended, the developments in science are recognisably 'Renaissance' in their methodology and the way they were financed and publicised. As in every other aspect of intellectual life, changes occurred which permanently altered both perceptions and ways of doing things. While one might suggest that 200 years is too long a period to be defined as 'a turning point', none the less, the Renaissance permanently changed most aspects of intellectual life, and many features of economics, government, religion and geography. These changes were much more than a new fashion in art or new discussion topics for students of politics and theology.

Questions

1. How significant to the ordinary people of Europe were the political and technological changes brought about during the Renaissance?
2. Discuss the view that the Renaissance can be better understood in terms of continuity than of revolutionary change.

SOURCES

1. RENAISSANCE CHANGES IN EUROPE

Source A: Dante explains the subject of the *Divine Comedy* in a letter to his patron Can Grande della Scala, *circa* 1314.

The subject of the whole work then, taken merely in the *literal* sense is 'the state of the soul after death straightforwardly affirmed', for the development of the whole work hinges on and about that. But if, indeed, the work is taken *allegorically*, its subject is: 'Man, as by good or ill deserts, in the exercise of his free choice, he becomes liable to rewarding or punishing Justice.'

Source B: Machiavelli on fortune, 1513.

Fortune is the ruler of half our actions but that she allows the other half or thereabouts to be governed by us . . . I would compare her to an impetuous river, that when turbulent inundates the plain, casts down trees and buildings, removes the earth from this side and places it on the other, everyone flees before it and everything yields to its fury without being able to oppose it, and yet, though it is of such a kind, still, when it is quiet, men can make provision against it by dykes and banks, so that when it rises it can either go into a canal, or its rush will not be so wild and dangerous. So it is with fortune.

Source C: Rabelais puts into the mouth of Gargantua a description of the perfect education, 1532–4.

I would have you model your Greek style on Plato's and your Latin on that of Cicero. Keep your memory well stocked with every tale from history . . . Of Civil Law I would have you learn the best texts by heart and relate them to the art of philosophy. And as for the knowledge of Nature's works, I should like you to give careful attention to that too … Then scrupulously peruse the books of the Greek Arabian and Latin Doctors once more … and by frequent dissections gain a perfect knowledge of that other world which is man. At some hours of the day also, begin to examine the Holy Scriptures. First the New Testament and the Epistles of the Apostles in Greek; and then the Old Testament in Hebrew. In short, let me find you a veritable abyss of knowledge.

Source D: Christopher Marlowe in *Tamburlaine* (1587–8).

[Nature] doth teach us all to have aspiring minds
Our souls whose faculties can comprehend
The wondrous architecture of the world
And measure every wandering planet's course
Still climbing after knowledge infinite
And always moving as the restless spheres
Will us, to wear ourselves and never rest.

Questions

1. Identify the evidence in Source D that Marlowe was familiar with the recent developments in the understanding of science. (2)
2. What new teachings on the subject of 'free choice' (Source A) emerged during the sixteenth century? (3)
3. What evidence can you find from the style and content of Source C to suggest that Rabelais is writing satirically? (5)
4. Compare the perceptions of life and religion offered by Sources A, B and D. To what extent do they offer a recognisably 'Renaissance' view? (7)
*5. Making use of your own knowledge, discuss the extent to which these sources suggest that the Renaissance was strictly the concern of the intellectual élite in Europe. (8)

Worked answer

*5. [This kind of question gives you an opportunity to put what you know about the whole period into a concise and structured answer, based firmly on the limited insights of the sources given.]

At the time of Dante's writing, patronage was an essential part of the artist's life. Dante was writing his epic account of Heaven, Hell and Purgatory on the orders and with the support of a wealthy patron. His work would not be printed until more than a century after it was written.

Thus few copies existed. Besides, the subject matter was not of every-day interest, even if multiple copies had existed and ordinary people had been able to read. Although it was written in Italian, it was not generally accessible. Machiavelli's irreligious views on fortune do not appear to have been shared by the mass of the population of Europe, if we judge by the enduring nature of superstition, and the many rituals, designed to placate God and to ensure His support, followed by the ordinary people across Europe. Rabelais's account of the perfect education, aside from being unattainable by any student, is clearly describing a full-time and expensive course of studies. Over much of Europe, basic grammar and literacy were being taught in towns, where guilds and religious foundations were able to collect sufficient students; but for the peasant population of Europe, this kind of education was both irrelevant and unattainable. Marlowe, however, was writing for a popular audience, though of necessity an urban one, and his lines would suggest that he thought that the questions of 'the wondrous architecture of the world' was a matter for 'us all'.

It is clear that the university level of education, like the expenses of artistic and architectural projects, were not available to the ordinary people. However, these few sources cannot show the extent to which ideas filtered down, and practical developments in fact changed the lives of the population, whether from having printed service books and Bibles to assist in their worship, from having new commodities and materials from other continents (after all, Elizabeth I's were not the only teeth to be ruined by the newly available, cheap and addictive sugar) or from a questioning approach which may have reduced the unthinking acceptance of authority.

SOURCES

2. PERCEPTIONS OF RENAISSANCE ART

Source E: Dante discusses (in the voice of Oderisi the artist) the transient nature of fame, ?1314.

O empty glory of man's frail ambition
How soon its topmost boughs their green must yield;
If no Dark Age succeed, what short fruition.

Once Cimabue thought to hold the field
In painting; Giotto's all the rage today;
The other's fame lies in the dust concealed.

Guido from Guido wrests our native bay,
And born, belike, already is that same
Shall chase both songsters from the next away.

Source F: Michelangelo Buonarroti to Giovanni da Pistoia, 1510.

My beard doth point to heaven, my scalp its place
Upon my shoulder finds; my chest, you'll say
A harpy's is; my paintbrush all the day
Doth rain a rich mosaic on my face . . .
In front to utmost length is stretched my skin
And wrinkled up in folds behind, while I
Am bent as bowmen bend a bow in Spain
No longer true or sane.

Source G: Michelangelo Buonarroti to Benedetto Varchi, 1547.

. . . and I now consider that painting and sculpture are one and the same thing
unless greater nobility be imparted by the necessity for a keener judgement,
greater difficulties of execution, stricter limitations and harder work.

Source H: Fynes Moryson on the Italians, 1601.

The Italians think themselves to have so much understanding and their country to
yield so much sweetness, fruitfulness and such monuments of arts and fabrics as
they seldom or never travel into foreign kingdoms, but driven by some necessity
either to follow the wars or to traffic abroad: this opinion that Italy doth afford
what can be seen or known in the world, makes them only have homebred
wisdom and the proud conceit of their own wits.

Questions

*1. What part of his career is Michelangelo describing in his poem (Source F)? (2)

2. Explain in your own words the reasons suggested by Michelangelo (Source G) to show that sculpture is of 'greater nobility' than painting. (3)

3. What, in the opinion of art historians, are the significant achievements of the two artists mentioned in Source E (Cimabue and Giotto)? How important was their work in the development of Renaissance art? (5)

4. With what justification did the Italians think as Fynes Moryson claims they did? (6)

5. By using your own knowledge, evaluate the extent to which

these sources convey an impression of the richness of artistic life in Renaissance Italy. (9)

Worked answer

*1. [A brief explanation as well as an answer will ensure that you collect both marks.]

This is a description of the painting of the Sistine Chapel ceiling. Although tradition has Michelangelo lying on his back at the top of the scaffolding, this and other sources suggest that he painted standing up but – obviously – leaning back in the contorted position of which he writes so tellingly.

NOTES AND SOURCES

1. THE BEGINNING OF THE RENAISSANCE

1 Charles Homer Haskins: *The Renaissance of the Twelfth Century* (Cleveland, 1957).
2 Ernest Gombrich: *In Search of Cultural History* (Oxford, 1969).
3 F.W. Kent and P. Simons (eds): *Patronage, Art and Society in Renaissance Italy* (Oxford, 1987).
4 Alison Brown: *The Renaissance* (London, 1988), p. 93.
5 Evelyn Welch: *Art and Society in Italy 1350–1500* (Oxford, 1997) p. 11.
6 Elizabeth Eisenstein: *The Printing Revolution in Early Modern Europe* (Cambridge, 1983).
7 Daniel Waley: *The Italian City Republics* (London, 1978).
8 Kent and Simons, op. cit.
9 Hans Baron: *The Crisis of the Early Italian Renaissance* (Princeton, 1966).
Source A: Evelyn Welch: op. cit., p. 125.
Source B: Alison Brown: op. cit., p. 95
Source C: Ibid., pp. 94–5.
Source D: J. Clements and Lorna Levant (eds): *Renaissance Letters* (New York, 1976), p. 9.
Source E: *The Portable Renaissance Reader* (New York, 1958), pp. 91–2.
Source F: Alison Brown: op. cit., p. 104.
Source G: Ibid., pp. 98–9.
Source H: Ibid., pp. 109–10.
Source I: Roy Porter and Mikulás Teich (eds): *The Renaissance in National Context* (Cambridge, 1992) p. 35.
Source J: J.H. Plumb (ed.): *The Penguin Book of the Renaissance* (London 1964), p. 143.

2. HUMANISM

1 Roberto Weiss (new edition by Ruth Rubinstein): *The Renaissance Discovery of Classical Antiquity* (Oxford, 1988), p. 203.
2 Ibid., p. 15.
3 Peter Murray and Linda Murray: *The Art of the Renaissance* (London, 1963) pp. 134–41.
4 Alison Brown: op. cit., p. 52.
Source A: Vasari: *Lives of the Artists, vol. II*, trans. by George Bull (London, 1987), pp. 1–2.
Source B: Peter Murray and Linda Murray: op. cit., pp. 8–9.
Source C: J.H. Plumb (ed.): op. cit., pp. 176–7.
Source D: C.E. Gilbert (ed.): *Italian Art 1400–1500 Sources and Documents* (Englewood Cliffs, NJ, 1980), pp. 157–8.
Source E: J. Clements and Lorna Levant (eds): op. cit., p. 18.
Source F: A.G. Dickens: *The Age of Humanism and Reformation* (London, 1977) p. 25.
Source G: Alison Brown: op. cit., pp. 106–7.
Source H: J. Clements and Lorna Levant (eds): op. cit., p. 11.
Source I: Ibid., p. 29.
Source J: Ibid., p. 33.

3. THE INFLUENCE OF THE RENAISSANCE ON MONARCHIES AND GOVERNMENTS

1 J. Clements and Lorna Levant (eds): op. cit., p. 249.
2 Desmond Seward: *Prince of the Renaissance* (London, 1974); Garrett Mattingley: *Renaissance Diplomacy* (London, 1955).
3 J.H. Eliot: *Imperial Spain* (London, 1965).
4 Desmond Seward: op. cit., p. 151.
5 A. Black and C. Black (eds): *Documents of British History* (London, 1920), pp. 331–2.
6 S.E. Lehmberg (ed.): *Thomas Elyot: The Book Named The Governor* (London, 1962), p. xiii.
7 G.R. Elton: *Policy and Police* (Cambridge, 1972), p. 190
8 Roland Bainton: *Here I Stand* (London, 1950), p. 61.
9 Antony Maczak in Roy Porter and Mikulás Teich (eds): op. cit., ch. 10.
Source A: J. Clements and Lorna Levant (eds): op. cit., p. 256.
Source B: J.W. Allen: *A History of Political Thought in the 16th century* (London, 1928), p. 25.
Source C: Ibid., p. 56.
Source D: J.H. Plumb: op. cit., pp. 152–3.

Source E: Ibid., pp. 153–4.
Source F: Daniel Waley: *The Italian City Republics* (London, 1978), p. 134.
Source G: M. Domandi (trans.): *'Ricordi'* (Philadelphia, 1965), pp. 44–5.
Source H: D. Chambers and J. Martineau: *Splendours of the Gonzaga* (London, 1981), p.15.
Source I: J. Clements and Lorna Levant (eds): op. cit., p. 303.

4. THE LINKS BETWEEN THE RENAISSANCE AND THE REFORMATION

1 Nicholas Davidson in Roy Porter and Mikulás Teich (eds): op. cit., pp. 47–8.
2 St Paul's Epistle to the Romans, ch. 5, v. 1, v. 18.
3 St Matthew, ch. 26, vv. 26 and 27; St Mark, ch. 14, vv. 22–5 and St Luke, ch. 22, vv. 19 and 20.
4 St John, ch. 6 v. 37, ch. 17, vv. 2, 6, 9, 24.
5 St Luke, ch.14, v. 23.
6 Donald R. Kelley in Roy Porter and Mikulás Teich (eds): op. cit., p. 137.
7 P.L. Rossi in S. Pumfrey, P.L. Rossi and M. Slawinski (eds): *Science, Culture and Popular Belief in Renaissance Europe* (Manchester, 1991), p. 149.
8 J. Clements and Lorna Levant: op. cit., p. 109.
9 St Luke, ch. 13, vv. 3 and 5.
10 A.G. Dickens: op. cit., p. 247.
11 St Mark, ch. 12, v. 17.
12 P. L. Rossi in S. Pumfrey, P.L. Rossi and M. Slawinski (eds): op. cit., p. 149.
13 Title of Luther's Tract, 1525.
14 A.G. Dickens: op. cit., p. 147.
15 Roland Bainton: op. cit., p. 41.
16 A.G. Dickens: op. cit., p. 147.
Source A: Dorothy L. Sayers and Barbara Reynolds (trans.): Dante: *Paradise* (London, 1962), pp. 128–9.
Source B: Myron P. Gilmore: *The World of Humanism* (New York, 1952), p. 192.
Source C: Roland Bainton: op. cit., p. 61.
Source D: Ibid., p. 124.
Source E: E. Cassirer, P.O. Kristeller and J.H. Randall (eds): *The Renaissance Philosophy of Man* (Chicago and London, 1948), pp. 224–5.
Source F: P. Partner: *Renaissance Rome 1500–1559* (Berkeley, 1976), p. 16 (i).

Source G: A.G. Dickens: op. cit., p. 124.
Source H: Myron P. Gilmore: op. cit., pp. 260–1.

5. THE LINKS BETWEEN THE RENAISSANCE AND OVERSEAS EXPLORATION

1 J.R. Hale: *Renaissance Exploration* (London 1965).
2 Carlo M. Cipolla: *European Expansion and Overseas Culture* (London, 1970).
3 Frederick Pohl: *Amerigo Vespucci, Pilot Major* (New York, 1944).
4 Genesis, ch. 1, v. 9.
5 Hans Koenig: *Columbus, His Enterprise* (London, 1976).
6 Felipe Fernandez-Armesto: *Columbus* (Oxford, 1992).
7 Bernal Diaz: *The Discovery and Conquest of New Spain*, trans. by J. Cohen (London, 1963).
8 G.C. Vaillant: *The Aztecs of Mexico* (London, 1950), p. 225.
9 J.H. Parry: *The Age of Reconnaissance* (London, 1963), p. 168.
10 J.A. Williamson: *The Cabot Voyages and Bristol Discovery under Henry VII* (London, 1961).
11 S.E. Morison: *The European Discovery of America: The Northern Voyages* (Oxford, 1971), p. 295.
12 D.W. Lomax: *The Reconquest of Spain* (London, 1978), p. 178.
13 David Birmingham: *A Concise History of Portugal* (Cambridge, 1993), p. 26.
14 Ibid., p. 28.
15 J.H. Elliot: op. cit.
16 Shakespeare: *The Tempest*, Act 1, sc. 2, l. 374.
Source A: G.R. Crone (ed. and trans.): *The Voyages of Cadamosto* (London, 1937), p. 5.
Source B: William C. Atkinson (trans.): *Camoens: The Lusiads* (London, 1952), p. 42.
Source C: W.D. Phillips and C.R. Phillips: *The World of Christopher Columbus* (Cambridge, 1992), p. 235.
Source D: C.W.R.D. Moseley (trans.): *The Travels of Sir John Mandeville* (London, 1983), pp. 127–30.
Source E: Jack Beeching (ed.): *Richard Hakluyt: Voyages and Discoveries* (London, 1972), pp. 49–51.
Source F: Ibid., p. 60.
Source G: D. Englander, D. Norman, R. O'Day and W.R. Owens (eds): *Culture and Belief in Europe 1450–1600, an Anthology of Sources* (Oxford, 1990), pp. 341–2.

6. SCIENTIFIC CHANGE IN THE RENAISSANCE

1 Christopher Marlowe: *Tamburlaine the Great*, Part 2, Act V, sc. 3 (London, 1590).
2 Luce Giard in S. Pumfrey, P.L. Rossi and M. Slawinski (eds): op. cit., p. 19.
3 A.C. Crombie: *Science, Art and Nature in Medieval and Modern Thought* (London, 1996), p. 103.
4 D. Englander, D. Norman, R. O'Day and W.R. Owens (eds): op. cit., pp. 338–42.
5 Traditional Bidding prayer at Christmas services.
6 Joseph Addison: *Hymns Ancient and Modern* (London, 1861), no. 662.
7 Richard Dawkins: *The Blind Watchmaker* (London, 1986).
8 Joan Solomon: *What Is Science?* (Hatfield, 1992).
9 Ibid., p. 23.
10 J.A. Bennett in S. Pumfrey, P.L. Rossi and M. Slawinski: op. cit., pp. 184–5.
11 Ibid., p. 172.
12 John Henry in Ibid., p. 201.
13 Ibid., p. 191.
Source A: Ivor B. Hart: *The World of Leonardo da Vinci* (London, 1961), p. 141.
Source B: J. Clements and Lorna Levant (eds): op. cit., p. 155.
Source C: S. Pumfrey, P.L. Rossi and M. Slawinski (eds): op. cit., p. 252.
Source D: J. Clements and Lorna Levant (eds): op. cit., pp. 178–9.
Source E: Evelyn Welch: op. cit., p. 90.
Source F: Ivor B. Hart: op. cit., p. 209.
Source G: J.H. Plumb: op. cit., p. 174.
Source H: S. Pumfrey, P.L. Rossi and M. Slawinski (eds): op. cit., pp. 193–4.

7. THE NORTHERN RENAISSANCE

1 Craig Harbison: *The Art of the Northern Renaissance* (London, 1995), p. 22.
2 Ibid.
3 Roy Porter and Mikulás Teich (eds): op. cit., p. 147.
Source A: Vasari: pp. 141.
Source B: E. Ruhmer: *Lucas Cranach the Elder* (London, 1963), p. 18.
Source C: Craig Harbison: op. cit., p. 155.
Source D: D. Englander, D. Norman, R. O'Day and W.R. Owens: op. cit., pp. 275 and 277.

Source E: Ibid., p. 40.
Source F: J.C. Collins (ed.): *Utopia by More* (Oxford, 1927), p. 15.
Source G: D. Englander, D. Norman, R. O'Day and W.R. Owens: op. cit., p. 230.
Source H: Shakespeare: *The Tempest*, Act V, sc. 1, ll. 181–4.

8. DID THE RENAISSANCE CHANGE EUROPE?

1 Roy Porter and Mikulás Teich (eds): op. cit.
2 Ibid., p. 1.
3 J.W. Allen: op. cit., p. xiv.
4 Christopher Frayling: *Strange Landscape* (London, 1995), p. 6.
5 Peter Murray and Linda Murray: op. cit., p. 276.
6 S Pumfrey, P.L. Rossi and M. Slawinski: op. cit., p. 61.
7 Ibid., p. 95.
8 Roy Porter and Mikulás Teich (eds): op. cit., p. 146.
9 Ibid., p. 5.
10 Evelyn Welch: op . cit., p. 221.
11 Carlo M. Cipolla: op. cit.
12 E.H. Gombrich: op. cit.
13 S. Pumfrey, P.L. Rossi and M. Slawinski: op. cit., p. 65.
Source A: Dorothy L. Sayers (trans.): *Dante: Hell*, (London, 1949) pp. 14–15.
Source B: N. Machiavelli: *The Prince* (London, 1954), ch. 18.
Source C: D. Englander, D. Norman, R. O'Day and W.R. Owens: op. cit., p. 92.
Source D: S.E. Morison: op. cit., p. 496.
Source E: Dorothy L. Sayers (trans.): *Dante: Purgatory* (London, 1955), pp. 152–3.
Source F: J. Clements and Lorna Levant (eds): op. cit., p. 106.
Source G: Ibid:, p. 122.
Source H: Carlo M. Cipolla: op cit., p. 24.

SELECT BIBLIOGRAPHY

COLLECTIONS OF PRIMARY SOURCES

David Englander, Diana Norman, Rosemary O'Day and W.R. Owens (eds): *Culture and Belief in Europe 1450–1600: An Anthology of Sources* (Oxford, 1990); J. Clements and Lorna Levant (eds): *Renaissance Letters* (New York, 1976); *The Portable Renaissance Reader* (London, 1977); Pamela Norris: *Come Live with Me and Be My Love (A Pageant of Renaissance Poetry and Painting)* (London, 1998). In addition, Vasari's *Lives of the Painters*, Cellini's *Autobiography*, Castiglione's *The Courtier*, and the writings of Machiavelli are among many primary sources available in the Penguin Classics series.

GENERAL BOOKS ON THE FIFTEENTH AND SIXTEENTH CENTURIES

The following books cover the period of the Renaissance, with developments put into context, particularly as far as politics and religion are concerned. Some useful books dealing specifically with the Renaissance are:

Alison Brown: *The Renaissance* (London, 1988); A.G. Dickens: *The Age of Humanism and Reformation* (London, 1977); Roy Porter and Mikulás Teich (eds): *The Renaissance in National Context* (Cambridge, 1992); E.H. Gombrich: *The Story of Art* (London, 1950); Peter Burke: *The Renaissance* (London, 1997); Robert Hole: *Renaissance Italy* (London,

1998); Evelyn Welch: *Art and Society in Italy 1350–1500* (Oxford, 1997); Peter Murray and Linda Murray: *The Art of the Renaissance* (London, 1963); Charles Nauert Junior: *Humanism and the Culture of the Renaissance* (Cambridge, 1996); Peter Denley: *The Italian Renaissance* (London, 1998); Lisa Jardine: *Worldly Goods* (London, 1996): focuses on the trade in art works, books, maps, etc., as well as money lending and credit.

RENAISSANCE EXPLORATION

There are many books, though few published since the modest flood which marked the Columbus quincentenary, such as Felipe Fernandez-Armesto: *Columbus* (Oxford, 1992), and C.R. Phillips: *The Worlds of Christopher Columbus* (Cambridge, 1992). Particularly useful are J.R. Parry: *The Age of Reconnaissance* (London, 1963) and *Spanish Seaborne Empire* (London, 1973); and C.R.R. Boxer: *Portuguese Seaborne Empire* (London, 1973).

RENAISSANCE SCIENCE

This area has been less well served, at least as far as the general reader is concerned. However, Marie Boas: *The Scientific Renaissance* (London, 1965) is accessible, and Stephen Pumphrey, Paolo L. Rossi and Maurice Slawinski (eds): *Science, Culture and Popular Belief in Renaissance Europe* (Manchester, 1991) is interesting, though not simple. The early part of Isaac Asimov: *A Short History of Chemistry* (London, 1972) is also relevant and readable.

THE RENAISSANCE OUTSIDE ITALY

This is dealt with in many of the books about the Renaissance cited above. Craig Harbison: *The Art of the Northern Renaissance* (London, 1995) has some very interesting ideas.

INDEX

94473